CA ... ERERS

On th ... masked men
brough ... es outside of
Mission, B.C. Minutes later, the masked ... ished into the
night with $7,000 and Canada's first train robbery was a matter of
record.

•

JACK (SAM) ROWLANDS

Sometimes the heavy iron box under Billy's seat was empty, but on
this trip it held $13,000 in gold dust and nuggets, and two gold bars
valued at $2,000.

•

ALMIGHTY VOICE

Almost out of ammunition, the brave pointed to Allen's gunbelt and
grunted. The inspector, feeling faint from loss of blood, shook his
head in refusal and waited for the inevitable bullet. The Cree was
about to jerk the trigger when a Mountie, seeing them, opened fire,
forcing Almighty Voice to flee for cover.

•

BULLDOG KELLY

A solid wall of white-hot pain slammed the packer as the bullet tore
into his hip. The concussion almost knocked him from the saddle but,
regaining his balance, the courageous halfbreed jerked his rifle from
its scabbard, levered a shell into the breech and fired, all in the same
motion.

•

THE WILD McLEANS

Drawing both pistols, he fired point blank, but, in his frenzy, missed.
Grabbing his musket, he jammed the barrel into the unarmed native's
midriff and jerked the trigger. The heavy ball slammed the old man
against the wall, killing him instantly.

•

SWIFT RUNNER

How could the stockings have found their way into an eye socket of
what was obviously a baby's skull? The answer, of course, was that
they had been placed there by human hands—if the hands of such a
monster could be called human.

Other *Stagecoach Books* by T.W. Paterson include:
  Ghost Towns of the Yukon
  Canadian Battles & Massacres
  Ghost Town Trails of Vancouver Island
  British Columbia Shipwrecks
  Hellship!

OUTLAWS
OF WESTERN CANADA

T.W. PATERSON

MR. PAPERBACK
LANGLEY, B.C.

MR. PAPERBACK
A division of
STAGECOACH PUBLISHING CO. LTD.
P.O. Box 3399, Langley, B.C. V3A 4R7

First Printing—August 1977

Canadian Cataloguing in Publication Data

Paterson, Thomas W., 1943-
    Outlaws of Western Canada

Bibliography: p.
ISBN 0-88983-008-8

1. Crime and criminals - The West,
Canadian - Biography. 2. Outlaws -
Biography. I. Title.
HV6805.P38   364.1'5'0922   C77-002160-3

COVER: The painting depicting Bill Miner and his gang performing Canada's first train robbery, was commissioned specifically for this book and painted by Manitoba artist, Terry McLean.

MR. PAPERBACK is a newly-created imprint, inaugurating a new publishing program that was conceived and designed to offer readers an inexpensive and attractive alternative to the higher-priced soft- and hard-cover books. It also presents an alternative to the pocket book, as the design and format bears a strong resemblance to regular-size books. This new imprint will feature original first printings as well as reprints of the more successful higher-priced books. *Mr. Paperback* is published by Stagecoach Publishing Co. Ltd.

...WANTED...

INTRODUCTION

Canadian outlaws?

The American interviewer was dumbfounded. Like tens of thousands of his countrymen, he had been raised on the wild west lore of movies and television, and the very idea that Canada had its own version of the wild and woolly west, with its own outlaws and lawmen, simply astounded him.

Several of our more colorful desperadoes, it must be admitted, had originally practised their trade below the border: "Bulldog" Kelly, Boone Helm, Bill Miner, Jack Dubois and the "Flying Dutchman." But others, such as the wild McLeans, Almighty Voice, Antoine Lucanage and Simon Gun-An-Noot, were native Canadians—and every bit as colorful and exciting as their American counterparts.

Certainly one of the greatest differences between the Canadian and American frontier was the establishment of the NWMP in 1873. Almost overnight, the lawlessness that existed on the Great Plains was ended north of the Medicine Line. It had been the debauchery of the Plains Indians which had prompted Prime Minister Sir John A. Macdonald to sign the order-in-council creating the red-coated police force.

This ravaging of the great native civilizations has been graphically described by a pioneer missionary: "Scores of thousands of buffalo robes and hundreds of thousands of wolf and fox skins and most of the best horses the Indians had were

7

taken south into Montana, and the chief article of barter for these was alcohol. In this traffic very many Indians were killed, and also quite a number of white men. (During the) winter of 1873/4, 42 able-bodied men were the victims among themselves, all slain in the drunken rows... There was no law but might. Some terrible scenes occurred when whole camps went on the spree, as was frequently the case, shooting, stabbing, killing, freezing, dying....

"Mothers lost their children. These were frozen to death or devoured by the myriad dogs of the camp. The birth-rate decreased and the poor red man was in a fair ways towards extinction, just because some men, coming out of Christian countries, and themselves the evolution of Christian civilization were now ruled by lust and greed. . . ."

The founding of the NWMP and its taming of the Canadian West is legendary. There were other police forces, such as the various provincial police, which played their parts in establishing law and order on the frontier.

Train robberies, stagecoach holdups, shoot-outs, lost loot and heroic lawmen: all were part of the Canadian frontier and contributed in their unique way to our heritage.   ●

1

BILL MINER

For all of the American—and Canadian—West's fabled outlaws, there never was another like Bill Miner, highwayman —and gentleman.

For half a century, and the better part of a lifetime, he plied his precarious trade across much of the continent, from the Deep South to the distant interior of British Columbia. When, finally, his incredible career came to a close in a prison hospital ward, Bill Miner left an unforgettable legacy as "the master criminal of the American West."

Just how Miner got his start in the business of holding up stagecoaches is not known although he staged his first robbery at the tender age of 16. Curiously, there is nothing in his childhood (at least as far as the records would indicate) to reveal just where young William A. Miner, of Bowling Green, Kentucky, went wrong. According to accepted legend, Bill left his father's ranch in 1859, when 16, to head west in search of fame and fortune. It was in California, with two companions, that Miner, the story goes, ran short of money and decided to rob a stage. When the venture proved to be a complete success, the tyro trio making good their escape with $75,000, the die, at least for Bill Miner, was cast.

Unfortunately for the gang, the money does not seem to have lasted long (Miner claiming, years after, that, as junior member of the team, he saw little of the loot) and they pulled a second job, then a third. It is known, however, that, despite his youth, Bill, if not the leader of the gang, was its mastermind and responsible for keeping all three robbers one step ahead of the posses searching for them; at least until they robbed one stage too many and were captured.

For Bill Miner, then 19, his arrest meant a sentence of three years in the hell-hole of San Quentin. Months later, tied to another robbery, his sentence was increased by a further two years. Not until the summer of 1870, after having served four years and three months in agonizing, brutal conditions, did he again know freedom.

For almost a year, nothing more was heard of the youthful highwayman who, it seemed, had learned his lesson within the grim walls of San Quentin. As it turned out, he had resumed his interrupted career with a vengeance. When stage after stage was held up, the robber escaping without leaving so much as a trace, authorities knew that they were up against a professional, although they could not be sure who. They did know that all of the robberies in question were staged by the same bandit, as all witnesses agreed upon one striking characteristic: the highwayman, throughout the holdup, behaved like a gentleman, speaking softly, courteously— almost apologetically—as he relieved the stages of their cash-box, the passengers of their wallets. It was to be a trademark of Bill Miner throughout the years.

For all of his courtesy, coolness and perseverance, however, Miner's luck had to fail him and, in June of 1871, just short of a year since his release from San Quentin, he again walked through the castellated iron gates of San Quentin, convicted of stage robbery. As before, his past came back to haunt him, Miner being tried and convicted of another robbery. This time, he faced a total of 13 hellish years in the pen; 13 years of unrelenting brutality and sub-human conditions. Unable to face the thought, Miner managed to escape, only to be recaptured within hours, whipped and thrown into the hole, a dark, dank and dungeon-like cell-block where the prison's hardest and toughest criminals were confined.

When he was at last allowed to return to his cell, it was to be kept under constant surveillance; a task made easier for his jailers by the fact that he now wore an "Oregon boot," a fiendish weight which was shackled to his leg and effectively reduced his chances of escape. Thus slowed to a shuffle, Bill had no choice but to behave and serve out his sentence. On July 14, 1880, after having served a total of 13 years in servitude, he strode through the gates of San Quentin, a free man.

But the Bill Miner of 1880, then 33-years-old, had not changed, let alone reformed. Rather than breaking his spirit, his years in prison had served only to harden his character and firm his resolve to defy the law. Perhaps, like the irrepressible Toad in *Wind in the Willows*, there was something about a stagecoach that simply could not be denied. Whereas Toad was a slave to speed, Bill Miner was addicted to the role of highwayman.

He did make one concession to practicality in that he decided to start afresh in the cooler climate of Colorado, where he was unknown. There, with the help of a fellow veteran named Bill Leroy, Miner took up where he had left off 13 years before, robbing stage after stage. The prospering partnership, alas, was severed when, after robbing the Del Norte stage of just under $4,000, an irate posse caught up with Leroy and ended his career rather abruptly with a length of rope.

Miner got the message and moved on, this time to Chicago, where, perhaps unnerved by Leroy's fate, he decided to play it cool by posing as a well-heeled mining man from California. Perhaps he even considered giving up his increasingly hazardous profession for the straight-and-narrow, only to become bored after several months of respectability. Unable to resist the old temptation, he returned to Denver, where, with a new partner, he avenged himself on the Del Norte stage by striking it again.

As before, a posse was soon on the trail, bullets flying. Despite the fact that both bandits had a head start, and enjoyed fast mounts, the lawmen were not to be denied, the outlaws being cornered in a canyon. Miner's accomplice evened the odds by wounding three of the posse with his Winchester, but, unable to break out of the trap, they were forced to hold cover while the lawmen awaited reinforcements. When the posse did move in, they found Miner's partner—but no Bill Miner. The Grey Fox had eluded them again, although it had been a close call.

As usual, after a particularly harrowing mission, Miner changed locale and lay low. Unfortunately, when he did go back to work, it was in his old stamping grounds of California, with the almost inevitable result. Convicted of robbing the Sonora stage of $4,000, Miner was returned to San Quentin, to face a sentence of 25 years.

For a lesser man, it could have proven a fatal blow; for Bill Miner, merely an inconvenience. Twenty years of misery later, he returned to society. He was 60-years-old, grey and grizzled. During a generation behind bars, not only had the century changed, but the world. No longer did stagecoaches form the lifeline of commerce; the American West of 1903 was criss-crossed with railroad tracks, virtually all freight—and shipments of money—being transported by train. This time, authorities were convinced, Bill Miner was finished. Old and tired, in a world of change, he was but a harmless throwback to the past. This time, they said, he would hang up his Winchester and bandana.

But they did not reckon with Bill Miner. Although the world had changed, he had not. With his old confidence, he willingly accepted the challenge of speedier communications and improved police efficiency. Undaunted in the face of technology, he simply changed his methods to suit the day, robbing, with two accomplices, the Oregon Railroad & Navigation Co. express, a few miles outside of Portland.

Miner's first attempt to keep up with the times almost proved to be his last. Although he and his companions succeeded in forcing the engineer at gunpoint to bring the train to a screeching halt, from that point on the script went awry. Bill Miner, stagecoach holdup artist extraordinaire, was out of his element with both trains and the dynamite with which he planned to blow off the doors to the express car. Instead, he almost demolished the baggage car with an over-charge, when a hardy express messenger opened fire and seriously wounded one of the robbers. At this point, Miner called the whole thing off and, thinking his accomplice dead, fled the scene with the other surviving bandit.

As it turned out, the wounded train robber not only survived, but talked. The third member of the gang was duly arrested, but the ringleader, now identified as the master highwayman, had once more vanished without a trail. Despite an intensive manhunt by Oregon and Washington authorities—and Bill's longtime nemesis, the Pinkertons—Bill Miner was gone, if not forgotten.

Although his hunters had no way of knowing, Bill had opted for more than a change of climate. For the first time in his lengthy career (although some American police records credit him with having been born in Canada), Miner had decided to try his luck outside of the United States, introducing himself to the settlers and ranchers of British Columbia's Nicola Valley as George Edwards, semi-retired American rancher.

With his easy-going manner and love of children, he became an immediate favorite with young and old. None who met the gray-haired Edwards, with his stiff moustache and commanding eyes, either disliked or forgot him. For, even at the age of 60, Miner cut a striking figure. Several years ago, former deputy commissioner of B.C. Provincial Police, Cecil Clark, described the famous highwayman from a wanted circular and photograph distributed by the Pinkertons.

Dressed in broad-rimmed hat and mackinaw, the aging man in the picture suggested an "honest sheep-herder in for a Saturday shopping expedition in some crossroads Montana town," wrote Clark. "His face, of course, is the main interest, and his eyes the most compelling feature. They have a look both direct and severe, enhanced perhaps by a slight furrow above the bridge of the nose. The nose by the way is longish and thin astride a sweeping moustache in the old cavalry tradition. The chin is pointed and a little bit unshaven, suggesting perhaps the start of an Imperial or a goatee.

"What's seen of his throat is a little in keeping with his apparent age; it's a little bit scrawny. The face is ascetically thin, the cheek bones high and you come back again to those masterful eyes. This, you feel, is a man born to command."

This was Bill Miner.

Apparently the American robber enjoyed independent means, despite the Oregon railway fiasco, for he made no serious effort to enhance his finances through honest endeavor; even managing, on one occasion, to drop $200 in a poker game in Ashcroft.

It is known, however, that he expressed great interest in local stage schedules, learning that the annual gold cleanup at nearby Bullion was to take place within days.

On the historic night of September 10, 1904, three masked men brought the CPR transcontinental to a halt several miles outside of Mission. As one held a Colt revolver to the engineer's head, locomotive 440 squealed to a stop, then, locomotive and express car unhitched from the rest of the train, engineer Nat Scott was politely instructed by the gang leader, a slender man in mackinaw and broad-rimmed stetson, to move the engine a mile or so up the track. There, at the threat of being dynamited, the express messenger unlocked the door. Minutes later, the masked marauders vanished into the night with $7,000, and Canada's first train robbery was a matter of record.

When, hours later, a manhunt was organized, it was already too late, Miner and accomplices having crossed the Fraser by boat and escaped to Bellingham, where the trail ended. Weeks after, the investigation ground to an inglorious halt. Not until a full year had passed, in November of 1905, were authorities reminded of the train-robbing trio when the Great Northern express was struck near Ballard, Wash. This time, the robbers escaped with $30,000. Although Miner was never officially tied to this holdup, at least one man, Seattle Pinkerton head P.K.

Ahearn, was convinced that the Ballard job boasted all of the earmarks of the longsought legend, Bill Miner.

During this period, the kindly, popular George Edwards had firmly established himself with Princeton residents, where he shared a ranch with another well-known oldster, Jack Budd. It was here that "Edwards" played host to his friends; particularly William "Shorty" Dunn, closemouthed sawmill hand who (at least, according to one source) was supposed to have killed a lawman somewhere in the American Southwest. But few asked questions about a man's past, and none questioned the affairs of Messrs. Edwards and Dunn, who came and went as they chose on several prospecting trips. Long after, when the friendly Mr. Edwards was revealed to be none other than the most wanted bandit of the day, locals recalled that, remarkably enough, both he and Dunn had been away on business at the time of the Ballard outrage.

As for Miner, he continued to bask in the role of retired rancher, and children's favorite, buying candy and entertaining local youngsters with his stories. Although friendly with all, it was noted that Edwards seemed to feel more at ease with children, subtly avoiding undue contact with adults and keeping pretty much to himself, with the exception of his constant companion, Shorty Dunn, and a second, newer acquaintance, Louis Colquhoun. Good-looking and goateed, Colquhoun had been a teacher, suffered from tuberculosis, and had spent much of his adulthood wandering across the country after a single conviction for petty theft. He, Edwards and Dunn became inseparable.

Late on the night of May 8, 1906, as the CPR locomotive No. 97 puffed and snorted through the darkness north of the tiny B.C. community of Ducks, engineer Callin suddenly found himself face to face with two masked and armed men, who clambered down from the coal tender and into his cab. Shoving his pistol into the startled engineer's face, one of the intruders gently asked him to stop the train. As the engine slowed in a cloud of escaping steam, a third man ran from the shadows. Moments later, at the outlaws' direction, the fireman uncoupled the locomotive and mail car from the rest of the train, when the gang leader ordered the engine and car several hundred feet farther down the track.

There, both mail clerks surrendered without a struggle, the outlaws boarded and began to search for the registered mail, only to realize, with a start, that they did not have the express car, but the baggage car. With an uncharacteristic curse, Miner searched the compartment, finding, for his troubles, the glorious sum of $15.50! In his haste, he overlooked several innocuous-looking parcels containing $40,000. Disgusted, Miner ordered the engineer to drive them several miles down the line, when the three bandits took their leave.

Of all Miner's jobs over the years, that of Ducks, B.C. was his worst disaster. He had miscalculated the train's cargo and left a distinct trail for his pursuers who, under command of the widely respected Const. W.L. Fernie, were soon hot on his heels. Using Indian trackers, Fernie was able to keep up the chase—helped by the fact that the outlaws were on foot, having lost their mounts! Despite every natural obstacle in the form of rock, hard ground and river, Fernie's trackers stayed with the outlaws' trail, until it became apparent that the wanted men were heading for the American border.

Finally, after stalking his quarry for miles, Fernie sighted three men and turned back to pass the word on to a NWMP patrol, which closed in on the three strangers as they were having lunch. Although the spokesman for their party, who introduced himself as George Edwards, laughed at the suggestion that they were train robbers, his coolness almost dissuading the policemen, the question became academic when Shorty Dunn panicked, pulled a revolver, and began blasting away. Seconds later, a bullet in the hip ended his short flight into the bush and the three men were taken into custody. A search of their campsite and clothing turned up a small arsenal in the form of five handguns and a rifle.

Days later, word of the arrest made international headlines when police learned that their prisoner named George Edwards was none other than Bill Miner, most wanted stage and train robber on the continent. Tried solely for the Ducks robbery, although other evidence indisputably linked him with the Mission holdup of two years before, Bill Miner was convicted, after the first jury ended in deadlock, and sentenced to life imprisonment in the penitentiary at New Westminster. For their part in the robbery, Dunn also received a life sentence (in deference to his having pulled a gun when arrested), the tubercular Colquhoun being let down with 25 years (ironically enough, a life sentence also as he died behind bars).

As far as the law, on both sides of the 49th parallel, was concerned, the case of Bill Miner, highwayman, was finally closed. Never again, they were sure, would he know freedom and the temptation to utter the words he had made famous: "Hands up."

But, as usual, the law had underestimated Mr. Miner. As a newspaperman had noted at his trial in Kamloops, Miner did not look anything like his age: "A rather striking looking fellow,

with grizzled hair and moustache, erect and active (he) doesn't
appear to be within 10 years of the age credited to him on
prison records. He claims to be 63, but looks like a man of 50,
and moves like one of 30."

Fourteen months later, while pushing a wheelbarrow in the
prison brickyard, Miner observed that, at one spot in the yard,
a tall smokestack obscured the tower guard's vision. Soon
Miner was hard at work, making frequent trips with loads of
bricks—to that enchanted spot where he could not be seen by
the guard. Enlisting the aid of three other convicts, he
succeeded in scratching a hole under the fence. Patiently, he
waited for the precise moment when, with his three comrades,
he slipped under the fence, scaled the prison wall, and
vanished into the woods.

Within minutes, the prison was in an uproar, guards in
pursuit. Miner's three accomplices were soon apprehended,
but of the old Grey Fox, not a trace. He never returned to
British Columbia, although it was a long time before provincial
police gave up the search, unaware that they could have saved
themselves the trouble as Miner, although at last feeling his
age and the years of privation behind bars, had turned his
attention to the eastern and southern states.

Four years after his escape from the B.C. Penitentiary,
Miner and two new recruits (throughout his career, he seems
to have favored gangs of three) boarded an express train near
White Sulphur, Georgia, and escaped with $60,000, thus
committing that state's first train robbery. But, this time, Bill's
past was to do him in. Later picked up for questioning because
he answered the description of the gang leader, Miner, calling
himself George Anderson, stoutly denied having anything to do
with the holdup. Unfortunately, among the officials questioning
him was a Pinkerton agent who took one look at the protesting
Mr. Anderson and identified him, from the agency's very
complete wanted circular, as the oldest highwayman in the
profession. This time, Bill's goose was cooked.

Sentenced to 20 years in Milledgeville State Prison, the
68-year-old robber was put to work in the prison farm. Seven
months later—he was gone!

With the help of a strong young fellow convict, Bill
overpowered a guard and slipped into the swamps. It was a
grand gesture, and almost his last. Old, enfeebled from more
than half a lifetime in prison, Bill just was not the man he once
had been. Two weeks later, exhausted, hungry and dishearten-
ed, the convicts sought shelter in a boxcar, unaware that they
had been recognized and the alarm raised. When lawmen
surrounded the car, both Miner and his companion answered

the demand for their surrender with pistol fire, Bill only giving up when the other was killed.

Returned to prison, Bill was shackled to a ball and chain. Eight short months after, with two cellmates, he sawed his way through the bars of his cell and hit the road again!

Sadly, it was his last escape. Too old and weak to hold out, he battled his way through swamps infested with snakes, mosquitoes and quicksand, only to fall into the arms of a waiting posse. He was so weakened by his latest ordeal that he was placed in the prison hospital. For a year, he fought to regain his strength. But the magic stamina was gone. On the evening of September 2, 1914, the notorious Bill Miner—"master criminal of the American West," and originator of the expression, "Hands up"—made his final escape from all worldly woes.

2

WILLIAM QUANTRILL

At 4 p.m., June 6, 1865, William Clarke Quantrill succumbed of wounds in a Louisville, Ky., military prison hospital. After more than four years of unparallelled savagery, the hated Confederate guerrilla leader was dead. Twenty-two years later, his remains were exhumed and positively identified by his mother as being those of Quantrill.

Yet, 50 years later, and thousands of miles distant, a Coal Harbor, Vancouver Island, caretaker was "recognized" as being Quantrill!

And many accept his subsequent "murder" as proof of his claim!

His story adds an intriguing chapter to one of the bloodiest legends in early American history.

John Sharp first gained wide attention in August of 1907, when the *Colonist* featured the story: "Guerrilla chief's home at Quatsino," in which it reported that Sharp, watchman of the West Vancouver Coal Company's property at Coal Harbor, had been indentified as the Confederate terrorist.

American businessman J. E. Duffy, "a member of the Michigan troop of cavalry which cut up Quantrell's (sic) force," met Sharp at Coal Harbor while there investigating timber limits. Sighting the old man on the beach, he stopped in surprise.

"Is that you, Quantrill, you damned old rascal!?"

"Come into the house," replied Sharp, and the two conversed for hours. Duffy later said Sharp had admitted to being Quantrill, and that they had discussed the dismemberment of his band, Sharp being keenly interested in the Union cavalryman's point of view.

No one seems to have remembered that, in 1865, deciding to fight fire with fire, the Union commander in Kentucky had hired a band of raiders under Capt. Edwin Terrill, whose men finally surprised Quantrill at a farm in southern Spencer County. Two guerillas were killed and Quantrill mortally wounded. If Duffy actually saw Quantrill or any other prisoner, it must have been later.

Whatever, Duffy told of Sharp's saying that, after the fatal skirmish, shot in the shoulder and bayonetted in the chest, he had escaped, riding 70 miles to safety.

Sharp said he was cared for by a Southern sympathizer and, upon recovery, had managed to reach South America and lived in Chile for some years. He returned to the U.S. to become a cowboy in Texas and Oregon. In 1897 he was in B.C., working in logging camps, and trapping, before settling at Coal Harbor.

Prior to Sharp's being "recognized" by Duffy, he had spoken of Civil War experiences, of having made a long ride while badly wounded, and of having been cared for by a quadroon girl. And rumors did exist that he was the notorious guerilla chieftain and had somehow escaped death in Kentucky.

The press stories prompted R. F. Montgomery of Quatsino to say he remembered Sharp from Fort Worth, Tex. Quatsino postmaster H. O. Bergh added he, too, had heard stories that Sharp was Quantrill and how he had survived being bayonetted in the chest and shot in the shoulder. Bergh had seen the scars.

Quantrill had been nearly six feet tall, had thick blond hair, grey-blue eyes, a down-curling mouth, very fine features with a "Roman nose," and was considered to be handsome. Almost all agreed that Sharp, then between 70 and 80 years of age, had probably answered to this description in his earlier years.

The late Sidney S. Saunders, former member of the B.C. Provincial Police, game warden, timber cruiser, prospector and First World War veteran, knew Sharp.

"I heard the story of John Sharp being Quantrill. It always interested me and I know many persons who were more intimate with him than I could possibly be, believed it. They did not say much. According to what I could learn, Sharp, when half-tanked, would boast of being the Southern leader, but when he was sober would resent any reference to the subject. He was an old man, as I recall him; about five feet 11 inches in

height, straight, wiry and active. He was possessed of
snapping blue eyes and a powerful voice.

"You will understand that it was no business of the B.C.
police if he was Quantrill. As far as our records went,
Quantrill had committed no offence against the laws of B.C. or
of Canada. It was no crime for him to fight against the Union in
the Civil War. It was curiosity on my part only.

"I would say that he was about the same age as Quantrill—
in other words, he was born about the same year. He was of
similar height and general appearance fitting the description
of Quantrill. It was known that his body bore marks of several
gunshot wounds, and a bayonet or knife cut."

Other witnesses reported Sharp was a crack shot with pistol
and rifle. Quantrill had been an excellent marksman.

The late Eustace Smith, a prominent forest engineer, met
Sharp in 1902, when he and his brother were acting as guides
to a wealthy hunting and fishing party in the Quatsino area.

"I was very interested in meeting him as I had heard it
whispered that he was Quantrill. He had steady blue eyes that
did not suggest a decline of his mental or physical reflexes. I
recall his powerful voice. I did not hear him admit to being
Quantrill, but from various remarks made while we were there
it would appear that he was a Civil War veteran and had
fought for the South. He spoke of Jesse James, the bandit, with
familiarity. Jesse James and his brother Frank were members
of Quantrill's band."

All connected with the mystery seem well-versed with the
history of Quantrill and his gang. Apparently the rumors
surrounding Sharp caused them to consult history books in the
hope of proving or disproving the conflicting claims.

One who knew Sharp well was a Quatsino resident, now
deceased. Upon telling of his part in the story some years ago,
he asked that his name be withheld, and will be referred to as
Mr. "G."

"Sharp was six feet tall, fine-featured with high cheek
bones, blue eyes, and had a ramrod-straight carriage. He was
the northern blond type," Mr. G. recounted. "If he'd donned a
shirt of mail, put on an eagle-winged helmet, he'd have looked
every inch a Viking.

"While Sharp fought with the Confederates, his speech
carried not the slightest Southern accent. (Quantrill was born
in Canal Dover, Ohio.) He is supposed to have had a Southern
uniform. I did not see it, but one man told me he had it. But it is
perhaps true, as his cap-and-ball pistols were of the type used
in the Civil War.

"I cannot think of Sharp as an inventor of tales. He did not talk much when sober, but after a few drinks, the Civil War was fought over again.

"These details are very clear in my mind to this day. I cannot recall a single incident Sharp ever told when we two were alone at his house, as he seemed to like a mature audience—and a dram of hootch—to restart the war."

But Mr. G., then very young, was present when Sharp told most of his adventures. The story of Sharp's escape is the most intriguing.

"I heard John tell this story one night at a gathering of men at Bergh's store on steamboat day. The Queen City brought our mail and freight. She was equipped with a bar, so Sharp and the others were in a good storytelling mood. Sharp related the last fight he was in. It must have been near the close of the war. Sharp was badly wounded and lying on the ground, left for dead. He claimed to have been bayonetted even after he had fallen. He did carry seven great scars from these wounds. A friend of mine saw them.

"He lay on the field until darkness and, finding himself alone, managed to get to a quadroon girl he knew who hid and nursed him. But before he was well she rushed to his hidden room and cried, 'Fly for your life, John Sharp. They are coming for you!' He lost no time in getting away.

"You will note that Sharp put the words into the girl's mouth—'John Sharp.' You would think that being mellow with good booze and in an unguarded moment he would have said ' Quantrill '—that is, if he really were that person. But, of course, this proves nothing. I think Sharp's story about the girl to be true.

"But to finish his story: After reaching New Orleans, he managed to get a berth on a ship bound for South America, and was there for seven years. I do not remember what country in South America."

If the Latin American part of Sharp's story is true, it would indicate he had been a guerilla of some importance, as the lesser-known members eventually were able to return home. Another time, Sharp boasted that a $2,000 reward had been placed on his head.

When Sharp had sobered after these "admissions," he was surly and would not discuss the subject further, switching instead to talk of his experiences in the woods.

Sharp reputedly told another man stories concerning the James brothers, anecdotes of the Civil War, and said he had gambled in earlier days (as Quantrill is supposed to have). He also told this man the same story of having been shot in a barnyard that Mr. G. has related. But to this man Sharp definitely mentioned it as having occurred in Kentucky.

Another Quatsino resident told of his encounter with Sharp, in which he heard of the notorious raid on Lawrence, Kan. "...He told me many incidents of the raiding in the Southern states, although I do not remember all the details. One story was of a raid on Lawrence, Kan., where a large number of people were killed. Sharp, or Quantrill, was always strong in pointing out, when he told this story, that although they killed many, not a woman or child was injured, and he was indignant regarding some histories (sic) accounts in respect to this raid."

With few exceptions, including encyclopedias, historians record that 150 men, women and children were killed in this most savage raid of the Civil War. Yet in his very factual *William Clarke Quantrill: His Life and Times*, author Albert Castel made no mention of the raiders having killed anyone other than males. It is known many of the victims definitely were not adults—children by anyone's standards, excepting Sharp's.

Whoever Sharp may have been, the popular account of his death is as violent as that of Quantrill's. Shortly after the newspaper stories appeared stating Quantrill, as John Sharp, was alive, he died as the result of a brutal beating—according to the tale.

Then began the greatest myth of John Sharp: a tale of a 40-year-long grudge and murder of vengeance. It has been written many times, but fascinating as it is, it just is not true.

According to the legend, two Americans who had suffered at the hands of Quantrill during the war, upon seeing newspapers claiming "Quantrill lives...!" journeyed northward on a mission of revenge.

The pair, "obviously Southerners," found Sharp at Coal Harbor and killed him. It was about the time they were fleeing southward, the story continues, that Mr. G. found Sharp in his cabin, gravely injured.

"The weapon was a three-quarter inch iron poker about two feet long," he recalled. "The marks of the poker were quite plain on his temples, there were grey hairs on the iron, and welts showing on Sharp's head."

A year or so later, he was dying, this time for real. Upon realizing the end was near, he requested his beloved dog, Toby, be shot and buried with him, which was done.

"There were not many at his funeral," said Mr. G., "perhaps a dozen, nearly all from Quatsino. In 1939 the air force bulldozed the site. No trace can be found now."

John Sharp or William Quantrill was indeed dead, and Provincial Police Const. Arthur Carter left Victoria to investigate what had become a mystery of grand proportions, as the story travelled throughout the northwest. With each telling the tale became even more exaggerated.

This cloud of exaggeration and honest error persists to this day. Few seem to remember that Constable Carter concluded Sharp died of "chronic alcoholism."

According to Mr. G., two Americans were suspected for a time. Perhaps this is how the legend of revenge originated.

Searching Sharp's few effects, Carter found two cap-and-ball Colt revolvers, the butts of which were engraved with the initials "W. C. Q.," which could have meant "William Clarke Quantrill." Carter also found several letters addressed to Quantrill. Sadly, what happened to these articles is not known today.

During a September, 1965, visit to Victoria, 85-year-old George Nordstrom of Quatsino was interviewed by a *Colonist* reporter concerning his part in the remarkable Sharp legend.

At that time, Nordstrom, who investigated Sharp's death as justice of the peace, said: "I am convinced that John Sharp was actually Jesse James."

He based his belief on information given him by his late father, who "knew of the gangs when they were operating in the Dakotas..."

When examining Sharp's meagre possessions, he found "nothing there to show his identity or prove his background. All we found was a portrait which we assumed was a picture of his son.

"Years later I saw a picture of a man called Dalton who claimed to have been Jesse James. He looked like the portrait that we found, and I think he was the son of old John Sharp," Nordstrom said.

Upon inspection of Sharp's body he discovered "it was riddled with wounds—bullet holes, sabre and bayonet wounds. Some of the wounds showed where he had been pierced by a three-cornered bayonet."

Today the mystery of Sharp's true identity remains as deep as in 1907. If he was not Quantrill, there can be little doubt that he was one of the guerrillas. He knew too much about their activities in Kansas and Missouri to have been anything else. And he did possess Quantrill's guns and letters. Then who was he?

No "John Sharp" appears on any of the enrollment rosters in existence. Most of the better known of Quantrill's men can be accounted for. Ed Terrill, the Yankee raider, was killed but weeks after capturing Quantrill.

Why did Sharp seek the isolation of Coal Harbor?

Why did he speak of his past only after his tongue had been loosened by whisky?

Is it coincidence that his description matched that of Quantrill?

Was he just a pathetic old man who borrowed the reputation of a desperado for a few months' precious limelight?

Why was he named as Quantrill by Duffy, a respected businessman with no known reason to lie? Was Duffy simply mistaken?

Was Sharp given the guns and letters by a dying Quantrill in a Kentucky farmhouse?

Like most questions concerning William Clarke Quantrill, "bloodiest man in American history," these probably will never be answered.   •

3

MATTHEW RODERICK

Twenty miles northwest of the U.S.-Canadian border town of Midway lies the site of the former boom town of Camp McKinney, B.C. Here, high in the hills above Rock Creek between the Kettle and Okanagan Rivers, Camp McKinney's main street, lined with saloons, a hotel and more saloons, bustled in hectic gold rush days.

British Columbia's fabulously rich gold fields had drawn prospectors from all over the North American continent. The main reason for all the town's activity—and very existence— was the nearby Cariboo Mine, richest lode in the region.

Every few months the mine's output was melted down to small gold bars for easier handling and taken by buckboard to the railway head, situated at Midway, where it was shipped to company headquarters, at Spokane, Wash. As only two Provincial Police officers, Chief Const. W. G. McMynn and Const. Ike C. Dinsmore, were responsible for the entire Boundary District, a mounted guard of trusted miners usually escorted the bullion to the train depot. A great deal of secrecy surrounded the gold's departure, as it was a great temptation to Camp McKinney's rougher citizens.

Occasionally a company official would take the gold himself, at which time a number of armed miners would be sworn in at the last possible moment to act as escort.

On the day of the robbery, Aug. 18, 1896, A. D. Keane was

mine superintendent. General Manager James Monoghan usually took out the gold but Keane, having some business in Midway, volunteered and, upon receiving instructions on shipping procedure at Midway, and precautions against being held up, he departed alone. In the back of his buckboard was a canvas bag containing three gold bars, one large, two small, and weighing approximately 656 ounces—valued today at almost $100,000.

Three miles east of Camp McKinney, around a sharp curve, a masked man with a Winchester rifle lay in wait for the approaching superintendent. Minutes later, he had disappeared into the dense brush beside the road with the precious sack.

Hurrying back to town, the shame-faced Keane notified mine officials and a full investigation was begun, as word was sent to police.

In charge of the manhunt until police could arrive, Manager Monoghan ordered the town checked to see if any of the miners were missing. One could not be accounted for: Matthew Roderick, a Seattle miner who had been laid up because of a back injury and was due to leave for Seattle.

Monoghan then hurried to the vicinity of the robbery. Inspecting the brush at the scene of the crime, his men found the remains of a camp fire and many footprints—but no robber.

That afternoon, Officers McMynn and Dinsmore arrived and took command. Soon they too were at the site of the holdup, when they conducted a second search of the area. It was they who found a patch of recently disturbed soil. Scratching away the dirt, they found the remains of some apples, egg shells and a whisky bottle—all pointing to the missing Roderick. For eggs were a rare and expensive commodity in isolated Camp McKinney, and the only eggs around had been those brought in for the ailing Roderick; as had been the apples. The whiskey was a brand rare to the area, and bottles bearing the same label were found only in the rubbish pile behind Roderick's shack.

Now sure of their man, and that he had escaped across the border into Washington State, the investigation ground to a halt. Circulars with full details were sent out, mostly to the U.S. Rewards totalling $3,500 were also posted.

Months later, with the aid of the Pinkerton Detective Agency, Roderick was found, living comfortably with his wife in Seattle. However, through secret surveillance, which included a woman detective becoming friendly with Roderick's wife, they could detect no obvious signs that he had or was spending beyond his means.

Finally Seattle authorities tipped Midway police that they were sure Roderick was preparing a trip east. Eagerly, provincial police officers asked themselves if this was the break they had been waiting for. If Roderick did not have the gold in Seattle it meant that he had probably cached it in the B.C. Interior and was now returning for it.

With a Pinkerton detective at his heels, Roderick left the train at Loomis, rented a horse—from the sheriff—and struck out for the Canadian border.

Through the cooperation of miners, mine officials, Indian guides and police, his progress towards Kettle Valley was easily noted, although the watchers were careful not to alarm the suspect.

Then, after swearing in the mine officials as special constables, Chief Const. McMynn and his small posse galloped in pursuit of the suspected bandit.

It was late in the afternoon of Oct. 26, 1896, and three months after the robbery, that preparations for the staking out of every trail to Bald Mountain, the area for which Roderick was headed, were completed. Far down the main trail were Thomas Graham and an Indian guide on one side, Supt. Keane on the other. Chief McMynn was stationed nearby.

Soon Graham sent Keane word via the Indian that he had spotted a lone horseman ascending the narrow trail. Dusk fell. Then it was 9 o'clock, before Keane heard someone approaching. But in the darkness he could see nothing. Tensely, in vain, he tried to pierce the enveloping gloom, as the sounds grew louder. Finally the outline of a horse and rider loomed up within a few feet of him, and he hoarsely whispered, "Is that you, Matt?"

The rider stopped abruptly and jumped from the saddle. Then a frightened Keane heard the lethal double-click of a Winchester being cocked, and his Colt barked once. As the pistol's report echoed through the valley, Keane lit a match and peered into the face of Matthew Roderick. The man was dead.

Arriving on the scene, Const. McMynn and the others searched the bloodied body. With the Winchester was a revolver; both badly rusted and covered with pine needles, as though they had been cached for some time. Strapped about Roderick's middle was a sturdy moneybelt. In his pockets were a Southern Pacific timetable, a piece of candle, some small change and a pair of goggles.

Of the missing gold there was not a trace. Keane's shot had not only ended Roderick's life but further investigation as well, for now no one alive knew the missing bullion's location.

When the local mines petered out, Camp McKinney died, as had so many boom towns before it. For many years it decayed in the wilderness until, in August, 1931, a forest fire scythed across the area and it was totally destroyed. But the site can still be easily located.

During the 1930s, and more recently, mining companies searched most of the region's abandoned mine shafts in search of overlooked ore, but discovered no trace of the Cariboo Mine's stolen bullion. And, although it is rumored that a map exists showing the gold's location, Matt Roderick's secret remains unsolved.   ●

4

JACK (SAM) ROWLANDS

The Rowlands saga began about 1880, when Jack, also known as Sam, decided to seek his fortune in booming British Columbia; crossing the border, according to one account, just ahead of an angry American posse. Why his presence was so urgently desired by the sheriff on the other side is not given, although spunky old Rowlands' later exploits might provide a clue.

However, once over the line, Jack seems to have settled down to the less demanding trade of prospecting. He followed this pursuit, with little apparent success, for the next 12 years. If he did not make his fortune, he did earn a reputation for being industrious, unassuming and honest.

Until July 19, 1892, that is, when Jack's halo slipped. Maybe he was getting hungry after all those years of chasing rainbows; perhaps it was the old call of adventure beckoning from the past. Whatever the reason, he returned to his early, evil ways—with a mask and a Winchester.

It was hot, that summer afternoon of 90 years ago, as Billy Parker urged his weary team along the dusty road near Post 98. Inside the jostling coach the single passenger, a hide buyer, watched the arid countryside in listless detachment.

The famous B.X. Company gave little thought to the dangers of road agents in those days. In isolated Cariboo country a bandit had little chance of escape. Sometimes the heavy iron box under Billy's seat was empty, but on this trip it held

$13,000 in gold dust and nuggets, and two gold bars valued at $2,000.

Billy gave his precious cargo hardly a thought as the bumping miles crept slowly by; he had carried this much and considerably more many times without incident—a fact which probably contributed to his state of shock when, suddenly, at the foot of Bridge Creek Hill, a masked man stepped from the jack-pine at the side of the trail and curtly ordered the lumbering stage to a halt.

From his perch, Billy looked down in awe at a short grey-haired man standing in the roadway—and right into the menacing muzzle of his rifle.

"Throw down that box!" the slight agent thundered, motioning evilly with his Winchester. When Parker numbly obeyed, the highwayman ordered him to proceed. Lashing his six horses, Parker charged on, leaving the robber and strongbox in his dusty wake.

A posse reached the scene hours later but there was not a trace of the robber or of the treasure chest. Rain had obliterated all tracks; he had vanished into thin air.

Word of the holdup and the outlaw's description was flashed eastward to Kamloops and to all southern points along the Cariboo Trail, down through Fraser Canyon. If the wanted man tried leaving the country by this route, the main road, he was sure to be noticed, leading police to believe he was still in the region, probably lying low in the woods. Posses doggedly scoured the wilderness without success. . . .

"Gold! They've struck gold on Scottie Creek!"

The hoarse cry shook Clinton like an earthquake. Men and boys frenziedly charged to the scene, 20 miles north of Ashcroft, as oldtimers scratched their heads in bewilderment. "Cain't figger it," said one. "Why, the creek's bin gone over with a fine-tooth comb. Even the Chinese gave up years ago."

But gold there was. Old Jack Rowlands, with a crew of two Chinese and two Indians, had struck paydirt after all those years of chasing the will-o'-wisp. Jack had established camp on Scottie Creek, a tributary of Bonaparte River, a month before, despite the knowing winks of townsfolk. Within three weeks he had proven them wrong, bringing out gold by the pouch.

From dawn till dusk, his sweating crew worked five ancient sluiceboxes. When days passed, then weeks, without his neighbors on the creek having any success beyond finding a little color, exuberant boasts and rumors gave way to ugly insinuation. Why was it, some asked in sarcastic tones, they worked as hard but found nothing, while Rowlands' camp added each day to its treasure?

Old Man Rowlands did nothing to discourage the doubters, making enemies of one and all by his marked hostility. Once he had been quiet, inoffensive, but now he was openly belligerent, warning all visitors off his claim at rifle point. He even ordered his men not to talk with the other miners if they valued their jobs—all very strange for a veteran member of the raucous mining fraternity.

Twice a week Rowlands forwarded a pouch of the coveted dust to storekeeper F. W. Foster's safe in Ashcroft by B.X. stage.

With each passing day—particularly the days Rowlands shipped his treasure—the miners became increasingly bitter. The most inexperienced youth in the luckless company knew something was decidedly wrong with the entire business.

Finally one man became angry enough to brave Rowlands' rifle and invective. Striding into camp, he approached the glowering miner and demanded to know why it could be no one else found gold although they had painstakingly searched every inch of creekbed. To his surprise, Rowlands answered; not politely, but he answered.

He had, he said, spent a month scouring Scottie Creek, looking under every rock and shifting tons of gravel without finding so much as a nugget. Until he found his present claim; it must be the mother lode, he reasoned.

When the miner reported back to his comrades, they discussed the grizzled prospector's explanation. The unanimous verdict was they'd never heard the likes of a creek which could be so rich in one little spot and totally barren everywhere else. With their verdict came a decision to inform the police of Scottie Creek's mysterious miner with the golden touch of King Midas.

Gus Erikson and Ed Wright were duly appointed to take the weird story to Ashcroft. Here, the miners earnestly told of the strange events on Scottie Creek. Constable Burr listened gravely but remained unimpressed. There just was not enough evidence to even prove a crime had been committed, he replied.

"Then how come Rowlands only finds his pile when his helpers are having dinner, eh? Answer us that!" challenged Wright. It was about then the skeptical policeman recalled the daring holdup of July 19. Fifteen thousand dollars, most of it in dust, was still missing. The only problem with this thought, however, as he patiently explained to his angry visitors, was the difficulty of identifying Rowlands' gold as being from the robbery, unless they could find the two bars.

Although pessimistic as to his chances of laying a charge,

Burr eventually agreed to return with Erikson and Wright, disguised as a prospector. Upon arrival, he joined those still panning the controversial creek, watching Rowlands' every move without being detected.

His surveillance confirmed the report that only Rowlands found color, always when his men were eating. Within days of the officer's arrival, it became apparent Rowlands was preparing to leave. Jack had paid off his crew and was bundling up his equipment when Burr and a crowd of miners called on him.

To the officer's question, he replied the claim was picked clean, he was pulling out. "No, sir, I'm afraid you're not," Burr answered. "I'm arresting you on suspicion of robbing the B.X. You'll have to come with me to Clinton to straighten this out."

A suddenly contrite Rowlands protested weakly, then surrendered without struggle.

When he finally faced a jury of his peers in a rustic courtroom packed with miners, it was to face a crown case of circumstantial evidence. Driver Billy Parker testified Rowlands was of the same build and age as the highwayman but he couldn't give a positive identification. As for the passenger, he sheepishly admitted he had seen nothing from his refuge on the coach floorboards after taking one look at the robber's rifle.

A more damning point was the remarkable coincidence concerning the date of the robbery and the time of Rowlands' first "strike." On July 21, but two days after Billy Parker threw down the strongbox to the man with a Winchester, old Jack had made his first deposit with storekeeper Foster.

Furthermore, declared the prosecution, Rowlands' claim had been thoroughly checked after his arrest, without a single grain of gold dust being found. To which the defendant sneered: "I cleaned it out."

But there was one piece of evidence Rowlands could not refute with a scornful laugh. Superintendent of Police Fred Hussey took the witness stand to deliver the coup de grace. A deathly silence fell upon the room as the mustachioed chief constable quietly explained how he and Const. Burr had impounded Rowlands' gold dust in Foster's store. Undramatically, Hussey told his spellbound audience how he and Burr had minutely examined the dust and nuggets under a powerful magnifying glass. Their inspection had revealed the gold could not possibly have come from Scottie Creek. At least, not all of it.

Every creekbed, he explained, left its own distinguishable mark on its gold. Usually washed down from the headwaters, nuggets were battered and polished by miles of swirling currents and abrasive bottom. The same would apply to gold taken from Scottie Creek. Instead, Rowlands' pokes contained nuggest and dust of all conditions. Some nuggets were worn smooth, others gnarled as if found near the source.

The gist of Hussey's testimony was that such an assortment of gold could only have come from many creekbeds—or the B.X. strongbox. The jury of miners did not need long to decide Mr. Rowlands had sluiced his fortune from the stage company, and the magistrate sentenced him to seven years in New Westminster penitentiary.

Two years later, Jack Rowlands was gone from the B.C. scene. Despite his advanced years, like that grand old highwayman Bill Miner, he had slipped out of prison and successfully eluded all pursuit. He was never seen again.

To this day, oldtimers around Clinton and Ashcroft wonder if Jack managed to return to his stashed loot before skipping across the border. Some maintain the hue and cry for his capture would have prevented his daring to reappear at Scottie Creek and vicinity where it is likely he hid the dust and ingots.

Which leaves the matter of $12,000 unresolved. The gold seized in Foster's safe amounted to $3,000. At today's prices, the remainder is valued at roughly $50,000.

Years after the famous robbery, surveyors laying out the route of the PGE Railway stumbled upon a rusted, battered strongbox in a brush-shrouded gulley, within five miles of Bridge Creek Hill. It was empty.   ●

5

AH-CHEE-WUN

Few would realize today that peaceful Pioneer Square is Victoria's last link with a series of brutal murders and a savage killer whose reign of terror was finally ended by roaring navy cannon and Royal Marines storming a Gulf Island beach head.

In Pioneer Square, where old men doze in the sun amid stately oaks and eroded monuments, where pigeons and gulls flutter noisily in search of crumbs, to the Sunday morning chime of cathedral bells, 15-year-old Caroline Harvey was laid to rest a century ago.

Ironically, while the tragedy began miles upcoast, the final scene was enacted but blocks away, in Bastion Square, where, July 4, 1863, before a crowd of wailing squaws and frowning braves, fate came full cycle.

"Intelligence was brought to town yesterday of as cold-blooded a murder as it has ever been in the province of a journalist to record," the *Colonist* reported, April 9, under the headline, "Horrible murder by Indians."

The chilling intelligence had been a breathtaking tale of treachery and miraculous escape told by a halfbreed Cherokee named John Henlee. He and his partner, Bill Brady, also American, had arrived in Victoria enroute to the Cariboo goldfields, when they decided upon a hunting expedition in the Gulf Islands.

Landing on a small island south of Salt Spring, Henlee had left Brady to cook supper while he hunted. Upon returning to camp shortly after dark, he found Brady entertaining visitors, three Cowichan braves and two squaws.

After dinner, all had retired; the miners to their tent, the natives, "who seemed very friendly," sleeping outside.

"In an hour's time, however, the sleepers were aroused by shots fired into the tent, by which both of them were wounded. Brady was rendered helpless, but Henlee, though hurt in three places, viz: one wound in the thigh and two in the left arm, fought the assassins with his uninjured fist. In the scuffle which ensued he received two severe cuts on the head from a squaw who attacked him with a knife, but he finally succeeded by dint of hard and well dealt blows, in making his antagonists run, when he seized his gun and fired after them, but with what effect he does not know."

Despite his own wounds, Henlee nursed his dying partner until the end, three days later. He then launched their whaleboat and began a painful, day-long voyage to town, landing at Oak Bay. Rushed to hospital, doctors removed a musket ball from his thigh and buckshot from his arm and groin, reporting him to be in serious condition.

Said the *Colonist:* "The public will anxiously look to the authorities for the institution of active measures for bringing the offenders to justice, as it is a subject that seriously affects the security of settlers in the outlying districts."

Sadly, it was just the beginning, for, the very next morning, headlines cried: "Another atrocious murder!"

This time the victims were German settler Frederick Marks and his married teen-aged daughter, Caroline Harvey. Their murder "vies in cold-blooded atrocity that which we chronicled in yesterday's issue," raged the newspaper.

The tragedy had begun with the 40-year-old homesteader accepting work on the Plumper Pass ranch of Christian Mayer. Loading the family possessions into two boats, Marks and Caroline had sailed northward in one, Mrs. Marks and their five younger children following in the second craft.

The little convoy had proceeded without incident to Saturna Island, when separated during a squall. Proceeding to Mayer's ranch, Mrs. Marks had inquired after the others, to be assured they would arrive shortly. But when hours passed without sign of the overdue couple, Mayer and an Indian employee returned to Saturna, to find "the debris of the boat and portions of a trunk, both of which had been hacked to pieces with an axe."

Searching frantically, Mayer found Marks' two dogs unharmed, "but every other article belonging to Mr. Marks had been stolen."

His helper had taken one look and exclaimed in Chinook, "The Cowichans have murdered them."

Hastening to Victoria, Mayer reported his grim discovery and told of "a certain bad Indian, who had been in the constant habit of boasting of exploits of this nature, and how little he cares for Gov. Douglas and the men-of-war. (Mayer's) Indian has told him that this ruffian, in company with several others, murdered three men at Plumper's Pass, in 1858, and sunk their canoe."

As fear of a general uprising swept the coast, authorities in Victoria urgently discussed the "reign of terror." Officials faced a temporary obstacle, however, in that no warships were immediately available, HM Gunboat *Forward* being at San Juan Island, HMS *Devastation* on a northern cruise, and HMS *Grappler* undergoing refit at Esquimalt.

The following day, *Forward*, under command of Lt.-Cmdr. the Hon. H.D. Lascelles, returned to Esquimalt to await further orders as Police Commissioner Augustus F. Pemberton conferred with Gov. James Douglas.

April 14, the *Forward* was still at Esquimalt, prompting a scathing *Colonist* editorial: "It is incomprehensible how the government can allow day by day to pass, without sending one of the gunboats to arrest the murderers. Both the *Forward* and the *Grappler* might have been dispatched on such a service; and, before the blood of their victims was dry; whilst their hands were reeking with human gore, and gloating over their fiendish deeds, the murderers might have been lodged in our prison."

When *Forward* finally made ready to sail, the newspaper sarcastically suggested: "She will probably get there in time to hear of a few more massacres."

Weeks passed with little word on the manhunt, but with reports of increasing Indian restlessness on both coasts of the Island, HMS *Forward* then returned to Victoria with Mrs. Marks and children, and three braves and a squaw suspected of being implicated in the Brady and Marks' murders.

Cmdr. Lascelles, with Police Supt. Horace Smith, had steamed first to Saturna to examine the Marks' camp, naval and police officers noting the smashed boats, a broken stove, and, on a rock, a pair of garters and a shoe. A torn, bloodstained petticoat was retrieved from the water, but neither Marks nor Caroline was found.

Cruising the Gulf of Georgia, investigators soon heard rumors that Lamalchi Indians had been responsible, shooting Marks as he sat by the fire, then chasing Caroline onto a rock where cruel hands held her as a squaw plunged a knife into her breast. Her body was then stripped, and thrown into the sea.

Days later, HMS *Forward* spotted several canoes returning from a potlatch at Chemainus. When officers approached in a gig, one canoeman pulled desperately for shore, bolting into the trees.

Cmdr. Lascelles immediately seized a chieftain in another canoe as hostage. Within an hour, villagers surrendered the fugitive, named Stalehum, who turned out to be the hostage's son and a prime suspect in the Brady slaying. Officers also found a second man suspected of the Marks' murders.

Proceeding up Sansum Narrows, *Forward* searched every canoe, bringing the frightened natives to with a shot fired overhead. But by this time, word had spread and no further suspects were located until *Forward* anchored in Kuper Island's Village Bay, home of the recalcitrant Lamalchi tribe.

From the deck, officers could see squaws hurrying into the forest with goods on their backs. When an interpreter hailed the village, two youths paddled alongside, to be told. "We want to communicate with the chief," one of the expedition later recounted.

"After waiting an hour we hailed them again and were told they would have nothing to do with us. After two or three ineffectual attempts to converse with them, the interpreters explained to them that they should have a quarter of an hour to send a chief to communicate, and, in the meantime, a red flag should be hoisted, which, when hauled down, was to be a signal that the gunboat would fire."

Hastening ashore with the ultimatum, the boys conferred with a chief. When they made to return to the ship, he stopped them at musket point, and those aboard *Forward* heard an old woman yell: "Don't go, they have come after the murderers but they won't get them."

When the time limit expired without further response, Cmdr. Lascelles ordered the flag lowered, at which all Indians still in view fled into the trees.

Forward then fired a warning shot over the woods, to be instantly answered by a devastating volley of musket fire from shore, Indians firing from behind rocks and trees, the gunboat answering with deadly belches of solid shot, shell, grapeshot and musket fire.

The duel continued without visible injury to either side for 90 minutes, when, suddenly, a seaman fell dead, shot through the temple.

Cmdr. Lascelles ordered his ship to cease fire, and as a

moody silence descended upon the island, again demanded an interview, and was again refused. After conferring with Supt. Smith, he decided to break off the engagement, spend the night at Chemainus and return in the morning.

When *Forward's* marines charged up the beach, they found Kuper Island deserted; not a man, woman or child was found. Ah-Chee-Wun had vanished. The frustrated gunboat then cruised southward, to meet with further failure. Disgusted, Lascelles joined HMS *Grappler* at Comox. Together, the men-o'-war steamed back to Kuper.

As before, when marines and bluejackets stormed the shore, they met with no resistance, although the invaders were amazed at the abandoned Lamalchi defences. "In the Block House, which had been strongly constructed of logs, properly morticed and loop-holed on three sides for musketry, they discovered one 24-pound shot, which had only penetrated the front wall. There were rifle pits all round, in which the Lamalchas (sic) hid themselves during the engagement. There were also regular rifle-pits constructed inside the Block House, covered over with thick plank."

The invaders then burned the village, "which was a large one," and all remaining canoes.

Proceeding to Pender Island, the warships met HMS *Devastation* and began a search for Brady's body. Following Stalehum's directions, they located the hapless miner's remains in Shark Cove. After an examination by Dr. Turnbull, Brady was formerly interred.

At Cowichan, through the influence of Bishop Demers, teenagers Kaisue and Swane-a-hya, and an old woman named Thask (meaning "a fly"), were taken into custody without resistance, villagers simply arguing that as but one white man had been slain, it was only fair that one Indian be tried.

Here, *Forward* picked up Mrs. Marks and family, returning to Victoria with the prisoners and with reports that the Lamalchis had gone into hiding on Galiano Island. Also included in Supt. Smith's report was a second reference to the dreaded Lamalchi chieftain, "who has not been caught, (and) boasts that Mr. Marks is the 11th white man he has killed."

His name was Ah-Chee-Wun, Smith's frightened informants had said, with an uneasy glance over their shoulders, and he was feared by Indians and whites alike. Reputed to be more than 100 summers old, he had the strength and appearance of a young man, was a deadly shot with a musket, "neither arrow nor bullet could harm him," and his enormous canoe "skimmed the water with the speed of the wind."

Others told how he could smell enemies from miles distant

and could walk through solid rock. "They believe...that whoever he threatens is doomed," said the *Colonist*, calling him "a perfect fiend."

At the preliminary hearing, John Henlee, still "suffering much," testified against Kaisue, Swane-a-hya, Thask and Stalehum.

In the meantime, Supt. Smith was busy recruiting a special police force for the planned invasion of Galiano Island, despite a report from the schooner *Royal Charlie* that the Lamalchis had returned to Kuper Island. The merchantman noted: "They were very insolent and said while the gunboat was firing they were lying in the woods looking at her and laughing at the *tenass* warship for wasting her powder and shot."

The Lamalchis even had had the audacity to order quarry workers off Salt Spring Island within a week or "they would cut all their throats."

When a number of halfbreeds enlisted to serve as guides on the forthcoming expedition balked at wages of $1 a day, Supt. Smith had had to prevail upon Commodore Spencer for additional bluejackets and marines from HMS *Devastation* and *Topaze*.

A week later, *Forward* and *Devastation* ended a second sweep of the Gulf Islands with another prisoner, several hostages and witnesses. The starving Lamalchi, separated from his tribe, had surrendered when the Cowichans refused him food. Also at Cowichan, Kaisue's wife, suspected of having instigated Brady's murder, gave herself up to settler John Humfries.

Early on the morning of May 23, Kaisue, Swane-a-hya and Stalehum, convicted of slaying Brady, mounted the gallows before the police barracks in Bastion Square, as 350 persons, mostly grieving Indians, watched silently. Minutes later, it was over. The sentence of the old squaw Thask had been commuted to life imprisonment.

When the gunboats completed yet another expedition, they had four more prisoners. But the dreaded Lamalchi "pirate chief," Ah-Chee-Wun, had again escaped the net. His capture, however, seemed imminent as all neighboring tribes "consider they have compromised themselves with him, and are bent upon having him."

Finally, on June 8, HMS *Forward* steamed back to Victoria with the "blood-thirsty villain" in irons. Surprisingly, the Lamalchi terror and two companions had been captured with little resistance at his secret cave on Galiano Island. The reign of terror was ended.

When the hated firebrand, "who has not by any means a

forbidding appearance, if we except the villainy which lurks in his piercing, wicked eye," took his turn in the dock before Chief Justice Cameron, it was to face an equally anti-climactic finale. Charged with the shooting of seaman Charles Glyddon aboard HMS *Forward* during the Kuper Island battle, he and companions pleaded not guilty, Ah-Chee-Wun testifying that he had not fired during the incident and that "his heart was very good towards white people."

After hearing the statements of Supt. Smith and the accused men, the jury retired. Two and a-half hours later, it found Ah-Chee-Wun, his brother Shanah-saluk, and Qualatultun guilty of Glyddon's death, recommending mercy. The following day, recommendation notwithstanding, Justice Cameron sentenced the three to death.

For the savage murder of Caroline Harvey, Um-whanuk was also sentenced to die. A fifth brave, convicted of manslaughter in the knifing of an unnamed white man "about five years" before, received four years at hard labor.

Because of Ah-Chee-Wun's conviction and sentence, two outstanding murder indictments, including that of Frederick Marks and daughter, were waived.

The final act of the tragedy came shortly after dawn in Bastion Square, July 4, 1863. As most Victorians prepared to celebrate the American holiday with friends from below the line with picnics, steamship excursions, parties and dances, "friends and relatives of the unhappy sufferers began to collect and set up a pitiable wail, which was continued until the closing scene of the tragedy."

Minutes later, the four hooded Lamalchis plunged earthward. For three, death was swift and merciful. But Ah-Chee-Wun, bloodthirsty terror of the Gulf Islands, jerked spasmodically "for about 20 minutes."

When at last he was still, the bodies were "handed to the friends of the deceased who conveyed them to the Indian reserve, and endeavored by all the arts they could exercise to restore animation to the lifeless corpses."

Earlier, the battered remains of Caroline Harvey had been found, stuffed in a crevice on Saturna Island, and interred in quiet Pioneer Square.　　　　　　　　　　　　　　　●

6

MOSES PAUL & PAUL SPINTLUM

CLINTON, May 3rd.—At a quarter to nine this morning a man rode into a temporary camp of the two Indian murderers Paul and Spintlum who are wanted for killing a man named White and a Chinaman who was a witness against them in his killing, both of which murders took place near Clinton last fall.

He recognized them but managed to leave their camp without arousing their suspicion and carried the alarm to a ranch house. The news was brought to Clinton immediately and a posse of six men left here at 11 o'clock headed by the local Provincial officer Alex. Kindness...

*　　　*　　　*

This 60-year-old news account from the Ashcroft *Journal* recalls one of the greatest manhunts in British Columbia history, the 18-month search for the Indian outlaws, Moses Paul and Paul Spintlum. Today, more than half a century after, this pair is remembered for the wild chase they led authorities.

Their amazing saga began in the summer of 1911 in the appropriately named Suicide Valley, south of Clinton, when fate brought together the first four actors of a tragedy which ultimately would involve hundreds of men, criss-cross hundreds of square miles of rangeland, and cost tens of thousands of dollars—and five lives—before the final scene was enacted in a Kamloops jailyard.

The first supporting actor was an elderly Chinese wood-

cutter and gardener named Ah Wye; the scene, his shack on
the historic Cariboo wagon road, just outside Clinton. The
second actor was a teamster named William White (who has
also been referred to as Alexander Whyte), who arrived at Ah
Wye's on the hot afternoon of July 4 to buy eggs. A third man
named Charlie Haller arrived with the same intent, when all
were joined by the star of the unfolding drama, 25-year-old,
mustachioed Moses Paul (also called Coxey Mowie) of the local
reserve.

The tragedy began uneventfully enough with White, Haller
and Paul enjoying a drink, and, shortly after, the three men left
Ah Wye's for Suicide Valley to consume the rest of their bottle.

Not until the next morning did the pace of our play pick up,
when teamster Louis Crosina, passing through Suicide Valley,
discovered White's battered body. Informed of Crosina's find,
provincial police constable John McMillan hastened to the
scene, to learn that White had been beaten to death with a
blunt object.

Although he found few clues at the scene, McMillan had no
difficulty in tracing the murdered man's last movements and
soon learned of his drinking bout with Charlie Haller and
Moses Paul. After questioning Ah Wye, McMillan concluded
that, having emptied their bottle, the three men had quarrelled
and fought, either Paul or Haller—or both of them—having
ended the argument with the bloodied rock found beside the
body.

Arresting Haller, the officer proceeded to Paul's shack to
question him, and, after a search of the cabin uncovered
White's watch, he charged the now sobered brave with
murder and locked him in the decrepit Clinton jail with Haller.

Brought before Magistrate Saul, both men were twice
remanded. However, on Aug. 12, Haller was released, Paul
being remanded a further eight days.

So far, the drama had proceeded almost routinely: Paul, or
Haller, murdered White, and McMillan arrested both of them.
But at this point the script went awry when McMillan made
two grave tactical errors, although quite understandable ones
under the circumstances. Firstly, he overlooked the security of
the Clinton lock-up. Secondly—and worse—he forgot about
Moses Paul's erstwhile friend, Paul Spintlum. In his 30's the
stocky Spintlum proved to be not only loyal but lethal,
possessing daring and determination—an unfortunate
strength of character, as authorities soon learned to their
regret.

The unholy alliance of the two Pauls was consummated
when Spintlum had a file smuggled into the jail in a baked

salmon, Paul soon rasping his way to freedom. On Aug. 15, joining Spintlum, he fled from Clinton to prompt one of the most trying manhunts in Cariboo history.

But before they vanished into the Cariboo hinterland six weeks later, the outlaws made an important stop at the cabin at Ah Wye. It had been the old woodcutter who had linked Paul with White in Suicide Valley, and the killer concluded that, with him out of the way, the Crown would have no case against him. Thus he cold-bloodedly removed the witness by splitting his head open with his own axe.

Although the inquest ruled that Ah Wye died as the result of "a blow of an axe, inflicted by a party or parties unknown," authorities entertained no doubts whatever as to Paul's guilt, and intensified their efforts to apprehend the outlaws. Weeks before, officials knew, Paul had secured a horse, rifle and ammunition. None doubted for a moment but that the manhunt would be difficult and, quite likely, deadly.

For, when Const. McMillan and his posse had galloped to Ah Wye's cabin, they realized that—if the events of preceding weeks had not been sufficient—they were up against two expert woodsmen. But for a few moccasin tracks about the murdered man's cabin, there was not a trace of the outlaws—Moses Paul and Paul Spintlum had vanished.

As retired deputy commissioner Cecil Clark of the B.C. Provincial Police noted several years ago: ". . .As successive generations of Cariboo lawmen will testify, it's no easy matter to run an Indian to earth in that part of the world. Especially if he has friends to supply him with grub and fresh horses. You can couple this to the fact that no foxier pair existed than Paul and Spintlum.

Consequently, despite the healthy rewards ($1,000 for Paul, $500 for Spintlum) offered by the authorities that October, fall and winter of 1911 passed without their capture. Then it was the spring of 1912. Previously, Const. McMillan had been replaced by Const. T. Lee of Savona, who, in turn, had been replaced by "Mr. A. Kindness, late of the Vancouver Provincial Police Force (sic)," as reported by the *Journal*, Dec. 23, 1911.

Thus it was that, on the morning of May 3, 1912, ranch hand Charles Truran stumbled into the wanted men's camp. As the *Journal* noted, Truran had immediately recognized them, but pretended to be unconcerned and "managed to leave their camp without arousing their suspicion." Then, whipping his horse about, Truran galloped back to his employer's ranch to give the alarm, when, alerted to the outlaws' campsite, Const. Kindness and a five-man posse charged in pursuit.

Accompanied by Const. Forrest Loring, George Carson, James Boyd, Bill Ritchie and Charles Truran, Kindness headed for the Pollard ranch, where Charles Pollard and his son John assumed the place of Truran, who had decided to retire.

For miles, the posse stalked its prey "through a heavy brush country," steadily gaining on the fugitives. After six miles, they overtook the pair's abandoned horses and camping gear. At this development, the posse took new heart, assuming that the outlaws had heard their approach, abandoned their exhausted horses, and proceeded on foot.

Constable Kindness and Loring approached the animals first, the others being just behind them on the trail. Kindness had drawn his rifle from its scabbard when suddenly, a shot shattered the stillness, one of the outlaws having fired from his hiding place behind a log. The bullet slammed into Kindness' chest, the atonished Loring reporting that his colleague doubled up in his saddle and, hands clutching his chest, cried, "Oh, you beggar!"

As more shots followed, Loring whipped his horse around and retreated for cover. Moments later, as he leaped from his horse, a bullet shattered his forearm. But, upon gaining the shelter of a tree, he drew his revolver and returned the outlaws' fire, when, upon seeing one of them jump from behind his log, "fired at him with (his) six-shooter, pursuing him for some distance as he ran.

"The posse were scattered in the dense brush and although several shots were fired at the murderers none took effect. On returning to the place where they were ambushed they found young Kindness laying on his back stone dead. He had been shot through the heart. It was useless to pursue the Indians in the dense foliage covering the hills, so the party divided, some staying to watch for possible signs of the murderers whilst the others came to Clinton for reinforcements."

Not surprisingly, word of Kindness' murder threw the town "into a great state of excitement," the *Journal* reporting that the young Scotsman, who had been assigned to Clinton but weeks before, had been "a fine specimen of manhood and deep regret is felt amongst his friends at the sudden taking off of such a promising young officer."

A fresh posse was immediately organized and dispatched to the ambush scene, but returned without accomplishing anything, as Const. W.L. Fernie arrived from Kamloops with a special detachment of Indian trackers which had participated, several years before, in the hunt for the notorious American train robber Bill Miner. In Clinton, most agreed that it would take at least "30 good men" to bring the killers to bay due to the fact that they obviously had been helped with food and ammunition by their friends, plus the fact that officers could expect Paul and Spintlum to fight to the death once they were cornered.

As the provincial government increased the rewards to $3,000 for both men (or $1,500 each, Spintlum now enjoying equal billing with Paul), Const. Fernie went to work. His first move was to arrest all relatives and friends of the fugitives, thereby reducing their hopes of securing provisions.

Then Fernie and his squad of veteran trackers hit the trail, following every lead. For three wearying weeks they hounded the outlaws, dogging their movements as Paul and Spintlum exhausted every trick in the book to throw them off. Slowly, the posse gained on the murderers, who were forced to abandon much of their equipment and supplies in a vain attempt to make better time.

Despite such tactics as the outlaws separating, utilizing the tracks of wild horses, and reversing the shoes of their ponies, the posse held on with the tenacity of bloodhounds. When the outlaws reached Bonaparte Creek, Fernie and company were right behind. But, at Kelly Lake, the killers reached harder ground and, finally, their trail petered out. For all of their efforts, the Indian trackers could not follow further and Fernie was forced to turn back.

By this time it was autumn once more, the manhunt having passed the year mark, with the outlaws still loose after two further killings. As 1912 neared its close, the authorities were desperate and decided to enlist the support of the region's Indian chieftains. To this effect, in mid-November, T.J. Cummiskey, Inspector of Indian Agencies at Vernon "summoned together three Indian chiefs at Clinton."

Writing of the meeting some six months after, Cummiskey termed the pow-wow "one of the most important events in the year's work," recalling that he had appealed to the tribal leaders "through a sense of justice and to their consistent belief in Christianity which I knew was implanted in their hearts by their missionary priests." After considerable discussion, much of it heated, and after noting that "It is not good policy in dealing with Indians to make a display of physical force and to fail—moral suasion is a better weapon," he convinced the chieftains to surrender the wanted men.

Thus, on Dec. 28, 1912, after a year-and a-half of pursuit. Moses Paul and Paul Spintlum were taken into custody without the firing of a single shot. After the months of bitter searching, through wilderness and in the worst of weather, their capture was anti-climactic, the *Journal* reporting that Indian agent

Cummiskey had employed something more than the "moral suasion" he had mentioned. According to the Ashcroft newspaper, Cummiskey had given the chieftains' the ultimatum that, if Paul and Spintlum were not handed over to the police by year's end, their "official dignities as chiefs would be cancelled." Whatever the agent's argument, it worked!

Brought to Ashcroft, Paul and Spintlum were said to be "somewhat emaciated (but) not in such a deplorable condition as might be expected from long exposure and hardships, and as they quietly smoked their cigars in the waiting room of the Ashcroft Hotel they did not seem like the desperate criminals which they really are. The captives left Ashcroft on the 4:30 train for Kamloops, where they will in all probability await trail at the spring assizes." Through the representation of their lawyer, Stuart Henderson (known as "Canada's Clarence Darrow"), the venue was changed to Vernon. However, despite extensive testimony by the members of the ill-fated posse on the day Const. Kindness was shot, and more circumstantial testimony, such as that of James Robinson who said that he had sold cartridges to Spintlum on the day that Paul broke jail, the jury disagreed and a new trial was ordered for the June Assizes at New Westminster.

This time the Crown offered overwhelming evidence and, on June 27, 1913, despite a "brilliant plea to the jury" by defence counsel Henderson, Paul Spintlum was found guilty of murder. Sentenced to hang on Sept. 12, Spintlum went to the gallows at Kamloops on Dec. 12, 1913.

Ironically, Moses Paul, the man responsible for setting the tragic chain of events in motion, was sentenced to life imprisonment, having been convicted on the lesser charge of accessory after the fact! As it turned out, Paul might just as well have been hanged, as he did not last long in prison, succumbing to tuberculosis. Most attribute his illness to the 18-month-long ordeal under trying conditions in the bush.

As a footnote to the tragedy, the provincial government struck silver medals for presentation to the chieftains who had been instrumental in surrendering the wanted men to justice. The leaders involved, however, resolutely refused to accept the honor and, but for an argument with agent Cummiskey as to the original terms of their agreement to turn in the fugitives, the amazing saga of Moses Paul and Paul Spintlum, murderers, was officially closed.

7

ONE-EAR CHARLIE BROWN

By anyone's standard, Charles H. 'One-Ear' Brown was a bad apple. A bootlegger, brawler, swindler and horsethief, this earlyday British Columbia desperado capped an infamous career with the ultimate crime, that of murder; an act for which he paid the supreme penalty after one of the wildest manhunts in provincial history. More than a century after, his date with justice is remembered as one of the very rare occasions of our past when vigilantes made their appearance —and subsequently were exonerated of criminal responsibility.

With such noteworthy contemporaries as the whisky-selling Livermores, John Butts, James Wright and others, Brown plied his nefarious trade on the forest fringes of shack-town Victoria, peddling "tangle-leg," or "snake head" (laced with lamp oil) whisky to thirsty natives in the villages cluttering the Inner Harbor's western shore.

And, like his contemporaries (perhaps we should say contemptibles!) Charlie became a frequent lodger in the grim castellated police barracks of Bastion Square, from which he would be escorted daily in the chain gang to repair city streets with six pounds of iron strapped to his leg. Upon release, he would be back to his old tricks. Bootlegging appears to have been his specialty, with a stab at swindling thrown in for good measure. Charlie, alas, differed from fellow tradesmen in that

he was a poor sport, usually resisting arrest violently until
overpowered, or at gunpoint.

His second recorded tilt with the law (the first—bootlegging
—having introduced him to the chain gang a year before)
occurred in September of 1860, when he was charged with
cheating his native clientele out of $20 with the promise of
buying them liquor. Upon the appointed hour, Charlie did not
appear with the promised refreshment and his outraged
customers reported him to the authorities, with the result that
Brown found himself in court. The magistrate, however,
dismissed the charge when one of the complainants failed to
appear.

But, exactly a week after, "on account of his inbred
propensities for swindling Indians," Charlie tumbled to three
months in the chain gang. He was out less than six weeks when
Sergeant Blake rapped on the door of his shack to inform him
that he was under arrest for selling a "can" of alcohol (10
gallons!) to a "Northern" Indian. Blake explained to the court
that he had had Brown and his former partner, John Jones,
under surveillance for some time but had been unable to clinch
the arrest until the previous evening.

A magnanimous magistrate offered Charlie a choice of 20
pounds sterling or three months, and it was not until the spring
of 1861 that his name again graced the court calendar. This
time, however, the charge was considerably more serious,
Charlie having been accused of resisting arrest by his nemesis,
Sgt. Blake.

At 3 o'clock the previous afternoon, Blake testified, he had
seen a man named John Guest driving a wagon toward the
harbor and, suspicious, he had followed the teamster with
Superintendent Smith. Crossing the bridge, Guest proceeded to
the Songhees reserve and to a rendezvous with Charlie Brown,
who, as Blake and Smith watched from the brush, unloaded a
case from the wagon and paid Guest some money. Brown then
"delivered the case to three or four Indians, who immediately
commenced breaking it open, and mounting the wagon (Brown)
rode off towards town with Guest."

Supt. Smith took off after the wagon, leaping into the back
just as Charlie jumped out "and showed fight." But, upon
looking into the forbidding muzzle of Smith's revolver, Brown
thought better of resisting and meekly surrendered. Sgt. Blake,
in the meantime, had his hands full with the Indians who had
attacked him with clubs and stones.

"He knocked one of them down with the butt-end of his
revolver and the balance fled," reported the *Colonist*. "The
sergeant made captive the Indian he had felled and took him to

prison with the whisky. While engaged in locking his prisoner up, an Indian, armed with a large dragoon pistol, rushed by the sentry at the door into the yard and attempted to shoot Blake. The latter knocked him down and locked him up. The would-be murderer is a Queen Charlotte Indian chief, named Eden-sah, and is well known as a bad character.

"Subsequently, John Guest was arrested on a charge of being an accomplice of Brown in his whisky business. The case will be heard this morning in the police court."

Such was the "whisky business" in Victoria, back in the good old days!

And such were the likes of Charlie Brown's business associates. As for Charlie, due to the lengthy proceedings involving Eden-sah's escapade, he was remanded until the following day when, with Guest, he appeared before Justices de Courcy, Pemberton and Brew. Appearing for their defence, counsel D.B. Ring opened his address on Brown's behalf with an appeal for mercy, saying that he "would not insult the court by attempting to rebut the plain, straight-forward evidence of the offence," that his client pleaded guilty and that he "asked mercy from the court, in order that he might have an opportunity of retrieving his lost character."

Alas, Ring's eloquent appeal fell upon deaf ears, Magistrate de Courcy replying that the bench felt no sympathy for Charlie. Further, said the judge, anyone convicted of selling, giving or putting liquor "in the way of Indians" could expect the maximum penalty, that virtually all crimes involving Indians were the result of liquor. Then, speech finished, de Courcy ordered Charlie to pay $500 or suffer 12 months at hard labor.

Brown's cohort, John Guest, fared considerably better when several citizens testified as to his high character. He, in turn, denied any knowledge of the contents of the crate and said that, as a "common carrier," he had merely followed the instructions of Brown, who had hired him to haul the case to Esquimalt. Despite his glowing references and staunch denial of complicity, the court found him guilty of being Charlie's partner in crime and fined him 20 pounds sterling.

As for Charlie, it can only be concluded that he coughed up his own hefty ransom as, not two months after, he was arrested—again—for bootlegging. This time Brown, "an intelligent-looking young man," faced a further charge of assault, the result of his having badly beaten a fellow prisoner, the Haida brave "Captain Jefferson."

Jailer Welch testified that Captain Jefferson had approached Brown in the jailyard "and said something to him about a schooner," at which Brown had jumped up and given "the poor

Indian a tremendous thrashing" before guards could haul him off.

"Guilty, your honor. But Jefferson came up to me first and said somethin' in Injun about a schooner, which I didn't understand, and kinder squared off at me; then I diffed him in the face, and he caught hold of me, and then I went into him and gave him a pounding—and a good one, too!"

Pemberton's reply to this defiant defence was to remand Charlie for three days, on bread and water.

Upon leaving the courtroom, situated in the police barracks, a reporter observed "poor Captain Jefferson, seated in a shady corner of the yard, and exhibiting a very dilapidated countenance. He informed us that Brown is the man who sold his tribe salt water for whisky, from the schooner *Laurel*, and that on accusing him with the offence, he had beat him most unmercifully."

All of which would indicate that, if nothing else, Charlie Brown was a busy man!

At any rate, he next appeared, with one "Hospital" Hall (said to be "a novice at the business"), before the bench to be convicted of selling a can of alcohol to an Indian, counsellor Ring again appearing in his behalf. Before sentencing, Brown pleaded with Pemberton, saying that, if released, he would leave the colony. Pemberton, however, was adamant, and replied that he would simply "prey upon (some) other community," and, as before, fined him 100 pounds sterling or a year in the chain gang. In deference to the fact that it was Hall's first offence, he was given the choice of 50 pounds sterling or six months.

This time Charlie could not cough up the fine and, once again, found himself with six pounds of iron shackled to his ankle. When the chain gang was ordered to work in the old cemetery, Charlie refused, and was placed on a diet of bread and water. Months after, tired of his stringent fare, he jumped jailer Edward Wright. The struggling guard unholstered his revolver and ordered him to desist or he would shoot.

Charlie's reply was to advance suddenly—and Wright fired. A moment later, "Mr. Brown's right ear was lying at his feet. The officer again cocked his weapon but, this time, there was no occasion to use it. The scientifically-cropped individual came to his senses, picked up the ear, and moved penitently to the new cell assigned him," the *Colonist* also observing that Brown "is represented to us to be very desperate and to have threatened the lives of officers before."

Then, adding insult to injury, Charlie faced trial on the charge of having assaulted Wright, the guard testifying that he had refused to change to another cell when ordered. "I...told him to leave his cell, which he refused to do unless the superintendent ordered him. He placed himself at the back of the cell; I put my hand on his shoulder and told him he must go. He then said, 'You—, if you lay your hand on me I will murder you!'

"He then laid hold of my arm." Wright continued, "and tore my shirt. After a struggle, he got outside the door and tried to shut me in. I prevented him, and held my pistol at his head and told him to go on. He went along the passage and then wheeled half round, upon which, thinking he was going to assault me, I fired at him..."

Found guilty (as usual), the mutilated Brown was handed another year, a reporter opining that "he has received a lesson which will keep him quiet for some time to come."

But Charlie—now known as 'One-Ear'—had not learned his lesson and, three months later, while being treated for an undisclosed (if not feigned) ailment in hospital, he made good his escape. Ten days after, despite an intensive manhunt, he had not been recaptured and the same journalist gleefully noted that he had been "a very troublesome customer and if he never returns the colony is fortunate to get rid of his presence so cheaply."

But if One-Ear Charlie Brown was gone from Victoria, he was far from finished. Worse, he was now beyond saving and, embittered by Victoria's inhospitable ways, he embarked upon a new career on the mainland as horsethief; a precarious profession which he followed sporadically for five years when, finally, he stole one horse too many and graduated to the dubious distinction of murderer.

Charlie appears to have been a considerably better horsethief than bootlegger, as it was not until 1867, after committing the unpardonable sin, that he at long last paid for his many sins. With the continuing excitement of gold mining, throughout the Cariboo and Kootenays, Charlie, upon fleeing from Victoria, headed eastward. Dipping below the border into Idaho, he prompted the final, blazing chapter of his career by stealing several horses from a ranch and heading northward for the new B.C. boomtown of Wild Horse Creek.

Here, on the bank of Stud Horse Creek, a shacktown had appeared almost overnight, as word flashed throughout the colony and below the 49th parallel that gold was being taken out in unbelievable quantities. Just how rich some of these claims were is revealed by the record which states that one Bob Dore made $7,000 in a single day's work! Other claims yielded up to $20,000 each during the summer months when work was possible, one company taking out an estimated $1,000,000 in a short season. Thousands, most of them American, flocked to the new Eldorados of Fisherville and Stud Horse Creek, since renamed Wild Horse Creek.

This was the brawling camp for which One-Ear Charlie Brown headed with his stolen horses. However, although he was unaware of the fact, the animals' owners, two stubborn Dutchmen, were in hot pursuit. For days, they followed the outlaw's trail until, finally, they came upon his camp near Fisherville.

Sensibly, they withdrew without attracting his attention and galloped into Wild Horse Creek to report to Constable Jack Lawson. An hour or so later, Lawson and his two guides rode into Brown on the trail.

Charlie instantly went for his gun but Lawson beat him to the draw and, finding himself staring into the business-end of Lawson's revolver, Charlie raised his hands. Tragically, at this instant, the young officer turned to call his companions. The unthinking motion took but a fraction of a second—just long enough for Brown to draw and fire, blowing off the back of Lawson's head. As his horse reared in alarm, Lawson pitched to the ground, dead.

At this, the Idaho ranchers retreated at full gallop, to report the slaying in Fisherville, where an excited populace listened to the news in growing rage. Back on the trail, Charlie relieved the dead policeman of his revolver and fled southward for the border.

Unlike Wild Horse Creek, which (until Lawson's murder) had boasted three constables, smaller Fisherville was not represented by the law. Consequently, when a four-man posse charged down the trail, armed and angry, all were miners. But what they lacked in legal authority they made up for in grim determination.

For hour after hour, mile after mile, they dogged Charlie's footsteps. Coming to the St. Mary's River, they learned that he had crossed by raft, and that the swift current had upset his float, costing the killer his outfit. This mishap had prompted Charlie to ask for a handout at the camp of Joe Davis, who hospitably had sent him on his way with a small stock of food. The obliging Davis then pointed out Charlie's trail to the posse which continued at the run, their lathering horses rapidly nearing exhaustion.

They were, however, rapidly gaining on the outlaw, who had abandoned his own mount. Also, aside from being short of grub, Charlie was running low on ammunition, apparently having lost his gunbelt in the river mishap; this, his pursuers surmised when they questioned a Chinese, who told how Brown had asked him for bullets.

Still the posse pressed on, the four miners refusing to turn back. Even when they realized that the Idaho border had been crossed, they galloped southward. Finally, at Bonner's Ferry, they met an Indian who informed them that a one-eared man had demanded ammunition on the other side of the Kootenay River.

With this, the miners realized that Charlie must be behind them, and, reigning their tired horses about, they charged back the way they had come. Hours after, beside the Walla Walla trail, and some 40 miles below the 49th parallel, they hid in the bush and waited. Reported the New Westminster *British Columbian*: "They soon saw him advancing at a rapid pace, with a remaining pistol in one hand and a knife in the other." Without warning, by common consent, three of the miners raised their double-barrelled shotguns and fired, "literally riddling his dastardly carcass."

The avengers left him where he lay beside the trail, until the following morning when they returned to bury him in a shallow grave.

Amazingly, although Brown's execution was the very antithesis of British justice (the fact it had occurred on American soil notwithstanding), even the authorities looked complacently, if not favorably, upon the vigilantes' act. A newspaper editorial aptly summed up the feelings of most British Columbians when it opined: "As a rule, we are not an admirer of Vigilante Committees...The Kootenay case (to which brief allusion is made by telegraph) seems to have been a terrible affair...

"That the constable of the district was shot and killed is undoubtedly correct. The murderer then appears to have made for the Boundary Line, to which he was pursued by the infuriated miners and killed. Ardent believers in law and order may deprecate the infliction of summary punishment by an unauthorized body; but we conceive that the executioners of the wretch Brown showed by the course they adopted a proper and just appreciation of the law.

"The magistrate was dead (referring to a report that the local magistrate had died in the midst of the crisis). Who was to issue a warrant? The constable was shot. Who was to pursue the assassin? Clearly, with the representatives of the law (and the) power of the Government lying dead before them, the right, the duty of the people was to prevent the flight of the evil-doer.

"They had to choose between the escape of the murderer

and his summary punishment. Aware that he was guilty of a capital offence in the eyes of the law, and well knowing that if he crossed the line he was safe from pursuit (the newspaper apparently thought that the shooting had occurred on Canadian soil), they decided to shoot him down. Paradoxical as the assertion may appear, when the miners took the law into their own hands and executed the criminal, they showed a high appreciation of that law and upheld its majesty."

A century after, Brown Creek, near Bonner's Ferry, recalls this exciting case: the day that vigilante justice ended the infamous career of One-Ear Charlie Brown, bootlegger, swindler, "thief and cowardly murderer."   ●

8

ALMIGHTY VOICE

In a century of "maintaining the right" from sea to sea, only six Royal Canadian Mounted Police officers have been killed by Indians. Of these, three were killed by a single Cree Brave named Almighty Voice during a chase that lasted for more than a year and a half.

A manhunt which ended in a "command performance" before a rapt audience of settlers and Indians, when a small army of North West Mounted Policemen, armed with field guns, finally brought the killer and his companions to bay...

Ironically, what was to become a tragedy of historic proportions began as no more than a misdemeanor, when, on Oct. 22, 1895, Sergeant Colin Colebrook arrested a young Cree brave for slaughtering a cow. Upon Almighty Voice's being secured in the Duck Lake guardroom, the affair should have been ended with a fine or minimal sentence.

But, sadly, the tragedy which was to claim seven lives, last 19 months, and make history, was just beginning.

If nothing else, the anonymous cow—its ownership remains in doubt—that Almighty Voice butchered must be one of the most expensive on record—making modern-day complaints against the inflated price of beef seem pale in comparison!

Perhaps the major mystery of the Almighty Voice tragedy is why the young Cree chose to escape. Perhaps he misunderstood the seriousness of the charge against him, thinking that he would be harshly punished. Whatever, that night, when a constable checked the little log guardhouse, Almighty Voice was gone.

However, if the slaughtering of a cow was a minor offence, escaping from custody was not and mustachioed Sgt. Colebrook headed in pursuit. He experienced no difficulty in tracing Almighty Voice back to the One Arrow Reserve. But there the trail seemed to end, the Cree tribesmen offering no information when questioned by the Mountie.

Not until a week after Almighty Voice's escape did Colebrook receive word that the brave was headed for his wife's home, Fort-a-la-Corne. Accompanied by a halfbreed scout named Francis Dumont, Colebrook followed at a gallop through a light snowfall, soon coming upon the trail of Almighty Voice, on horseback, and that of his 13-year-old squaw, on foot.

For miles, Colebrook and Dumont dogged their trail. Apparently sure that he was not being followed, Almighty Voice made no attempt to hide their tracks, the white crust of snow preserving their footprints clearly and enabling their pursuers to gain steadily upon them.

Finally, on the chill morning of October 29, Colebrook and Dumont spotted their quarry, the sergeant proceeding ahead of his scout. A veteran of the Riel Rebellion, and well versed in handling Indian lawbreakers, the officer jogged toward the startled couple.

At his approach, Almighty Voice raised his rifle, warning Colebrook to turn back. The sergeant, according to one account, continued his advance, his right hand raised in a sign of peace, his left clutching his service revolver, which he had placed in his overcoat pocket.

Again, Almighty Voice ordered him back, Dumont, who had been following Colebrook, obeying, and shouting to him to stop. But the sergeant ignored the threat, when, in a lightning move, Almighty Voice aimed and fired at a range of 10 yards, the heavy slug striking Colebrook in the neck, literally blowing him from the saddle, and killing him instantly.

At this, Dumont spurred his horse about and retreated, leaving Almighty Voice, his child-bride, and Colebrook's body where it lay. Although accounts differ in minor details, some referring to a shotgun, others to a rifle, and placing Colebrook's fatal wound as being in the neck, and in the chest, all agree upon the result of that seconds-long drama enacted upon a lonely, snow-shrouded prairie: Almighty Voice, wanted for no more than killing a cow and escaping custody, had killed a Mountie. The die was cast, there could be no turning back.

Sadly, the tragedy was to claim further lives before it was ended...

With Dumont's galloping off for help, Almighty Voice wasted no time in fleeing—on Colebrook's mount—after abandoning his bride beside the Mountie's body.

Alas, for poor Sgt. Colin Colebrook, insult was added to injury when he was posthumously criticized for having attempted to approach Almighty Voice alone, another officer expressing the opinion that he was "a brave Mountie in wanting to take his man alive but made a grave error in not keeping Dumont with him to hold a parley with the Indian. With a good explanation he would probably have surrendered."

Whether or not this would have been the case, no one, of course, can be sure. The fact remained that, for Almighty Voice, it was too late for speculation. Despite a clean record prior to the cattle-killing incident and jailbreak, he was now a killer. He could not expect the Mounties, who were sure to follow, to make Colebrook's mistake.

When Dumont breathlessly reported the shooting, police patrols swept the prairie, searching out all of Almighty Voice's known friends and relatives, and following up every lead. But, despite their every effort, and despite a most detailed description of the slayer, Almighty Voice was not to be taken.

There would be no mistaking the fugitive once cornered, as the Mounties enjoyed a complete description, right down to his "feminine appearance." For, curiously, Almighty Voice's countenance and bearing belied what he had become, police circulars describing him as "about 22 years old, 5 ft. 10 in. in height, weight 11 stone, slightly built and erect; neat small feet and hands; complexion inclined to be fair, wavy dark hair to shoulders, large dark eyes, broad forehead, sharp features and parrot nose with flat tip, scar on left cheek running from mouth towards left ear, feminine appearance."

Neither this description, nor the posting of a $500 reward (advertised against Commissioner Herchmer's wishes) resulted in a single solid clue as to Almighty Voice's whereabouts. Weeks of exhaustive investigation passed, police checking every lead, no matter how slim, nor how distant, inquiry even being made below the border. Then months began to creep by. Then a year. Sooner or later, they knew he would give himself away. When he did, they would be waiting.

As the Mounties were painfully aware, the credit for Almighty Voice's vanishing act went to his relatives and friends, without whose assistance he would never have lasted a month. Despite almost constant surveillance, and surprise "visits" to the One Arrow Reserve (not to mention many false leads, several of them undoubtedly the handiwork of the fugitive's protectors), police were unsuccessful. Ironically, Almighty Voice was virtually underfoot, for, throughout the months-long manhunt, he did not stray from his home hunting grounds. Even the $500 reward, posted six months after the slaying of Sgt. Colebrook, failed to inspire a Judas among his friends.

Then it was October 29, 1896—the anniversary of Colebrook's murder. But no Almighty Voice. Throughout these months of frustration and embarrassment for the force that always got its man, criticism of the Mounties' inability to bring Almighty Voice to bay grew. Finally an exasperated Commissioner William Herchmer lashed out at critics, drawing their attention to the two-years-long search for Ned Kelly, the "wild colonial boy," by Australian police. Snapped Herchmer: "If the Australian police sometimes have such trouble to arrest white men with the advantage of moderate weather all the time, how much more difficult it must be for the Mounted Police to follow and arrest an Indian in an equally difficult country surrounded on all sides by his own relatives and with the climate we have to contend with."

The great manhunt slipped into high gear two months after, on May 26, when Metis rancher Napoleon Venne, who owned a small spread adjacent to the One Arrow Reserve, surprised some Indians in the act of butchering one of his steers. Upon reporting the incident to police, Venne and Cpl. Bowridge returned to the scene. Although cattle killing was almost commonplace, if illegal, Cpl. Bowridge had been intrigued by Venne's having tentatively identified one of the threesome who had ridden from his slaughtered steer as Little Salteaux—cousin of the elusive Almighty Voice. Although Venne could not be sure, he thought that the second man might have been named Dubling, one of the much-married murderer's former brothers-in-law.

Bowridge could not conceal his excitement at this surprise development. For it did not take a detective to surmise that if two of the three rustlers were related to Almighty Voice by blood and marriage, was it not conceivable that the third member of the gang was the wanted man himself?

Upon reaching the One Arrow Reserve, Bowridge questioned several tribesmen, learning that Dubling had been there the night before to borrow a rifle. On the subject of Almighty Voice, there was a deathly silence for reply.

It was as they left the camp that the Mountie and rancher spotted two Indian riders attempting to conceal themselves in a grove of poplars. Suspicious, Bowridge and Venne slowly approached the island of trees. Rifles drawn, the men ambled forward until almost into the poplars, when a rifle exploded in their faces, the slug tearing into Venne's left shoulder.

Stunned by the impact and pain, Venne swayed in the saddle, almost falling, as his assailant rushed forward to dismount him. As the assassin—Almighty Voice!—reached for his horse, the stunned rancher, with a supreme effort, reined his horse about and, spurring it in retreat, galloped to safety. Although the Cree fired again, his second shot succeeded only in ventilating Venne's hat.

The drama had lasted but seconds. Upon Venne's being shot, Bowridge had opened fire, attempting to pin down the two men in the trees. As Venne galloped out of range, the Mountie forced the attackers to take cover with a departing shot, then led Venne to medical aid.

When word of this latest act in the Almighty Voice case was relayed to Prince Albert, Insp. John Beresford Allan, the courageous Irish veteran of the American Civil War, and the famed Sudan campaign, took personal command of the manhunt. With almost a dozen men of "F" Division, Allan rushed to the scene of the latest shooting.

The day after Bowridge and Venne encountered the phantom Almighty Voice, Insp. Allan's task force closed upon the outlaws, having had little difficulty in picking up their trail in the Minnichinas Hills. Upon spotting the Indians—three of them—ahead, the Mounties charged in pursuit.

However, when the Indians reached the cover of a large stand of poplars, Allan ordered his men to halt, instructing Sgt. C.C. Raven to station his men about the grove. When all were in position, Raven and a constable volunteered to establish the fugitives' hiding places by engaging them in gunfire.

This, they proceeded to do by entering the trees from the far side. Guns drawn, they moved stealthily forward, watching for the slightest movement, when, too late, Raven spotted the fugitives. Before he could warn his partner or shoot, the outlaws opened fire, a rifle slug smashing Raven's hip as the Indians fled deeper into the brush.

Upon hearing the gunfire, and alarmed for the safety of the two Mounties who had entered the grove, Insp. Allan ordered his men to mount up and charge. Almost instantly, Allan was the first to be hit and unsaddled. Shot in the shoulder, he crashed heavily to the ground—just as Almighty Voice, intent upon stealing his gunbelt, raced towards him, Winchester at the ready.

Stunned, Allan said afterward, he lay on his side, unable to use his shattered right arm or to stand upright. For a minute or two, he considered his situation, then began to pull himself, by using branches and roots, to a stump, where he was able to stand up—to find himself staring into the muzzle of Almighty Voice's old fashioned Winchester.

Almost out of ammunition, the brave pointed to Allan's gunbelt and grunted. The inspector, feeling faint from loss of blood, shook his head in refusal and waited for the inevitable bullet. The Cree was about to jerk the trigger when a Mountie, seeing them, opened fire, forcing Almighty Voice to flee for cover.

As the Indians retreated deeper into the brush, the Mounties withdrew with their wounded, an officer rushing to Batoche for medical aid and reinforcements, Cpl. C.H.S. Hockin assuming command of the seige.

When the reinforcements arrived in the form of more mounted policemen and civilian volunteers, Allan was taken by wagon to a nearby farm house, where police surgeon Hugh Bain removed "a heaped saucerful of splintered bone" from his right arm. Courageously, the inspector refused a drink of brandy, preferring instead to merely grit his teeth during the painful operation. Upon Dr. Bain's dressing the wound, Allan calmly asked for his pipe.

Back at the seige, Cpl. Hockin decided to smoke the outlaws out into the open, instructing his men to fire the poplars. But, as it was spring, the wood was too green and refused to burn. The outlaws had won round two.

Undaunted Cpl. Hockin decided to forsake prudence for dispatch—a fatal, foolish and unforgiveable mistake. For there was no question but that the Indians were trapped and had no hope of breaking through the police lines, even under the cover of darkness. All the Mounties had to do was to wait until hunger and thirst forced Almighty Voice and his comrades to either surrender or make a suicidal charge.

Sadly, it was Cpl. Hockin who chose to make the suicidal rush. With eight constables, and Ernest Grundy, Duck Lake postmaster and former policeman, Hockin mounted his horse and charged. Galloping blindly toward the trees, the 10 men fired wildly in hopes of keeping the outlaws pinned down. But, well concealed in the undergrowth, the Indians were able to return their fire with impunity—and with deadly effect, their volley cutting down Cpl. Hockin, Const. J.R. Kerr, and postmaster Grundy. Grundy and Kerr died instantly, Hockin was mortally wounded. The outlaws were untouched.

Just then, one of the Indians, named Tupean, stood up to take better aim at a horseman, when he, too, was shot dead. Thus, when the Mounties beat a bloody retreat, leaving their dead behind them, the half-time score stood at: Indians 3, Mounties 1.

At dusk, Supt. S. Gagnon reached the scene with eight men, to take up a night-long vigil. In the meantime, a specially chartered train, carrying Assistant Commissioner J.H. McIllree, 24 officers—and a nine-pounder gun—had puffed from Regina to Duck Lake in less than seven hours. Hours later, the field gun was in position, along with an old brass seven-pounder brought from Prince Albert, and McIllree's small army waited impatiently for dawn—and the final act of the drama.

In the trees, Almighty Voice and his surviving companion, Little Salteaux, also waited for the dawn. Against them were almost 100 men and two cannon. This time, they knew, there was no escaping.

By this time, also, Almighty Voice must have been resigned to his fate. About midnight, he taunted his enemies crying: "Brothers, we've had a good fight today. I've worked hard and am hungry. You have plenty of grub; send me in some. Tomorrow we'll finish the fight!"

Commissioner McIllree answered with several rounds of artillery fire. Then all was silent as each man settled back to wait for morning, the Mounties unaware that Almighty Voice had been wounded in the leg by shrapnel.

May 30, 1897, dawned bright and clear—and with an audience. For, as the sun rose, hundreds of persons—Indians, halfbreeds and settlers—gathered to watch the fatal performance.

With a roar, and a banshee wail, the first shells landed in the trees, as, from a nearby bluff overlooking the scene, Almighty Voice's mother chanted her son's death-song. Again and again the nine-pounder belched fire and smoke, the seven-pounder joining in a duet of death that Commissioner Herchmer later termed "most excellent practice."

Finally, at McIllree's signal, the guns fell silent. As an eerie stillness settled upon the land, from their vantagepoints, the audience watched in awe as the Mounties slowly advanced in a ragged line, then suddenly burst into a charge. But there were no shots fired. The battle was over.

When officers found the bodies of Almighty Voice and Little Salteaux, killed by shrapnel, they discovered that the Indians had dug themselves a shallow trench. Mute evidence of their thirst was given by the trunks of several saplings, the outlaws having stripped away the green bark which they sucked for moisture.

Then the police had carried away their dead, and the case of Almighty Voice, which had begun with no more than a slaughtered steer, was officially closed. The final count: seven lives. ●

9

CHARCOAL

Even as one of the wildest manhunts ever witnessed on the Canadian prairie was being conducted for the capture of the Indian outlaw, Almighty Voice, the NWMP found themselves with another killer on the run. What made the case of the Blood warrior, Charcoal, unique was the fact that, upon taking flight, he took his entire family with him, lodge-pole and baggage. At that, he almost made it!

Like so many other tragedies, that of Charcoal began as a domestic dispute, when a reckless young brave named Medicine Pipe Stem began courting Pretty Wolverine. Not only was Pretty Wolverine married to Charcoal, being the younger of his two wives, but she was a close blood relation to her lover. Both were sins that the middle-aged Charcoal could not overlook, and he repeatedly warned Medicine Pipe Stem to keep away from his wife.

But the younger man ignored him. A braggart and a bully who had served time in a NWMP jail for stealing horses, he continued to see Pretty Woverine whenever an opportunity presented itself. Their last rendezvous, on the afternoon of Oct. 13, 1896, was in the barn of a rancher named Cochrane. However, this time the lovers were not alone. Within minutes of their arrival, and their first embrace, Charcoal burst into the barn, rifle in hand, and shot Medicine Pipe Stem dead.

Moments later, as Pretty Wolverine fled to their lodge, Charcoal left his victim's body sprawled halfway through the doorway of the barn, and went on the warpath.

Just what prompted him to go in search of further victims is a matter of conjecture. Perhaps he felt that it was better to die as a lion than as a lamb, and to settle old scores before he was captured or killed in the chase that was sure to follow. The fact remains that, previous to his provoked slaying of Medicine Pipe Stem, Charcoal (despite his tribal name, Bad Young Man) had led a quiet, respectable life, and was said to be of "intelligence far beyond the usual," as well as a superb athlete.

But, with his wife's lover dead, Charcoal was determined to have blood and, for his next victim, chose Chief Red Crow who, in his mind, symbolized the Indians' surrender to the white man. Fortunately for the chieftain, who spent the month of Charcoal's rampage sleeping on the floor, he was not to be found and Charcoal, after telling Little Pine of Medicine Pipe Stem's death, turned to the local Indian agent, James Wilson. Again, he was thwarted when the agent proved to be unavailable and, in growing anger, the gunman proceeded to the home of the reserve's farm instructor, E. McNeill. This time, he was not to be denied. Upon spotting McNeill standing beside a table, he fired through the window. The bullet tore into the instructor's side and threw him to the floor, when Charcoal, not bothering to see if he was dead, hurried off to collect his family and begin his flight.

"Perhaps no other outlaw in the history of the West," marvelled writer Frank Anderson some years ago, "carried so much baggage with him as did Charcoal. In addition to Pretty Wolverine, he took along his second wife, Sleeping Woman, a grown daughter, his two teen-age sons and—incredibly—one of his mothers-in-law! Loading all personal belongings and tents onto the horses, Charcoal led the weird band of fugitives away from the settlement..."

Word of the shootings of Medicine Pipe Stem and McNeill spread rapidly throughout the Cardston reserve and, in short order, reached the ears of Agent Wilson (who, but for his lucky absence when Charcoal called, might have been one of the first to know—with fatal results). Inspector McNeill had also been found, lying where Charcoal had left him, and alive. As he was given emergency treatment, the NWMP were duly notified of the shootings.

Insp. A.M. "Buz" Jarvis immediately took charge of the manhunt; leading a police detachment to the Blood reserve, as Charcoal, complete with family entourage, attempted to put as many miles between himself and his pursuers as possible.

Amazingly, he did just that—despite his being encumbered with his large family, personal effects and a two-month supply of provisions. Within a few miles of where they picked up his tracks, Indian and NWMP lost his trail and were forced to turn back.

Two days after the shooting of Medicine Pipe Stem and McNeil, a coroner's jury returned a verdict of murder, and a warrant was issued for Charcoal's arrest. The trick of capturing him, as all involved were by this time aware, was another matter, and his description was circulated throughout the region. As a result, Inspectors Jarvis and H.J.A. Davidson received word that the fugitive had been sighted, some 15 miles west of Stand-Off.

Again, the police mounted up and galloped in pursuit. When overtaken by darkness, they camped beside the trail, then pulled out at daybreak.

Their tip soon turned out to be accurate as, upon coming to a 500-acre wood, they spotted the fugitives' tracks. Charcoal and his family had obviously taken cover in the trees and the Mounties removed their boots so as to approach the outlaw's camp on foot.

This stratagem, while effective, soon proved to be extremely uncomfortable, as the lawmen pushed on through the dense growth. Hour after hour, they forged onward in a skirmish line, without sighting Charcoal's camp. Unfortunately, the outlaw heard them when one of the Mounties, not as light-footed as his fellows, stepped on a twig and it snapped with a loud crackle.

Just a few yards ahead, Charcoal, who was in his teepee, heard the breaking twig and rushed outside. Spotting the Mounties closing in, he immediately grabbed up his Winchester and snapped off a shot at Insp. Jarvis, who was in the lead. Taking cover, the police responded with a volley before Jarvis, alarmed for the safety of the outlaw's family, could order them to cease firing.

The immediate lull enabled Charcoal, Pretty Woverine, Sleeping Woman and one of his sons to slip into the trees on the opposite side of the tents and, by the time Jarvis and his men could storm the camp, both were gone; the disgusted Mounties having to content themselves with capturing the rest of his family, and all of his supplies. Moments later, they were rejoined by Insp. Davidson's men, who had circled around the camp from the west. These tactics notwithstanding, Charcoal, his two wives and son succeeded in eluding them—after stealing the posse's horses.

Then, despite an ever-widening manhunt, as hundreds of cowboys and ranchers joined the search, the manhunt ground to a halt. Two weeks passed without a sign of the fugitives, when Supt. Sam Steele decided to try a different tack. Well aware that Charcoal was being aided and abetted by his relatives on the reserve, Steele ordered his men to arrest 25 relatives and friends, who were escorted to Fort Macleod and locked in the guard house. Two weeks later, Steele conferred with Charcoal's brothers, Left Hand and Bear's Back Bone, offering them their freedom if they would help in Charcoal's capture. If they refused they would be returned to the guard house, where all would remain until the outlaw was either killed or taken. Begrudgingly, the brothers agreed and were released.

The very next night, Cpl. William Archer of the Cardston detachment was checking the stable, lantern in hand, when a bullet passed under his outstretched arm. Luckily for Archer, he was only nicked, but the gunman, thought to be Charcoal, escaped into the darkness.

During the following 10 days, Charcoal became a will-o'-wisp; being sighted first here, then there, as he apparently made regular forays onto the Piegan reserve. Finally came word that his trail had been picked up near Beaver Creek, and Sgt. William Brocke Wilde charged in pursuit with a handful of men.

Courageous to the point of being foolhardy, Sgt. Wilde was not a man to let anything stand in the way of an arrest. To him, Charcoal was just another killer, and hardly to be considered a challenge. After all, it was Wilde who had single-handedly made Chief Piapot, the Cree "Lord of Heaven and Earth" recognize the might of the NWMP. Piapot had attempted to delay construction of the CPR by removing survey stakes, then having his tribe camp across the right-of-way. The only Mountie available had been Cpl. William Brock Wilde, an ex-Guardsman, who immediately rode into the Creek camp and gave Piapot 15 minutes to clear the site. When the time expired, and ignoring the threats and guns of Piapot's braves, Wilde stalked through the camp, kicking out the centre poles of each and every teepee, and collapsing the lodges upon their outraged occupants. But, for all of their anger, the Crees were impressed with Wilde's bravery, and humbly did as ordered.

Late in the afternoon of November 10, in deep snow and gathering gloom, Wilde and his posse overtook a lone rider with two horses. The lawmen had covered 30 miles since leaving Pincher Creek, and both men and mounts were exhausted. When the strange horseman suddenly switched mounts, then urged his fresh animal onward, they knew it to be Charcoal and Wilde whipped his weary horse forward. As all animals high-stepped through the snow, the sergeant slowly overtook the fugitive—when Wilde unaccountably disregarded his own order that Charcoal, if he refused to surrender, was to be shot at 50 yards' range.

Steadily, the posse fell behind, until only Wilde was still in the chase, and rapidly gaining on the Indian. Charles Holloway, the posse's interpreter, became alarmed at the situation and shouted to Wilde to stop. Contemptuously, Charcoal urged his pursuer onward. As the distance between the outlaw and the sergeant continued to close, Holloway jumped off his horse and aimed his rifle at Charcoal, who was about 100 yards distant. But his gun, its breech frozen solid in the cold, misfired twice.

At this moment, a fourth actor joined the unfolding tragedy. John Brotton, a settler, was out rounding up stray cattle when he chanced upon the impending duel. Within 50 yards of Charcoal and Wilde, he watched, enthralled, as the sergeant closed with his quarry. With the same disregard for the Indian that he had shown that day in Chief Piapot's camp, Wilde had rested his carbine—pointing away from Charcoal—across his saddle, his revolver remaining in its holster.

Charcoal seemed to ignore him, not turning to look back, even as the policeman came abreast of him on his left side. Then, as Wilde reached for his arm, Charcoal wheeled in the saddle and fired his rifle point-blank, the bullet entering Wilde's right side and coming to rest in his left glove, where it was later recovered. As Wilde slumped to the ground, Charcoal levered another shell into the breech of his Winchester (which obviously had not frozen) and, singing and shouting, shot the policeman in the stomach. He then seized his victim's horse and rifle and, after a defiant wave of his hat, vanished in the dusk. Tail Feathers, one of the killer's tribesmen who was acting as a police scout, immediately traded his own horse for that of Charcoal, and followed him into the gloom, towards the mountains.

The rest of the posse, upon seeing that there was nothing they could do for Wilde, resumed the hunt; trailing Charcoal throughout the night. By the next day, they were close enough to exchange shots with him, when the killer sought refuge in some trees. With nightfall, he was surrounded, but, some time before dawn, he again slipped from the trap. He did, however, leave a trail, which led off in the direction of the Blood Reserve.

About 3 o'clock that morning, Charcoal reached the home of Left Hand, his brother. After arousing the family, he stood at the door until Left Hand drowsily appeared and invited him inside. He was about to enter when, still on the threshold, something warned him of danger. With an oath, he backed outside and headed for his horse, Left Hand at his heels. When Bear's Back Bone appeared, Left Hand leaped onto his brother, hugging him about the chest and pinioning his arms, as he shouted to Bear's Back Bone for help.

Although exhausted after his long flight, Charcoal fought with the fury of a wounded bear. But it was no use and, moments later, his brothers wrestled him to the ground and tied him up. They then hauled him into the house, and placed him on the floor, with a blanket about him, as word of his capture was sent to the police.

While they waited, Charcoal sulked in the corner, his head on his chest, and deathly still. When one of his brothers, becoming suspicious of his frozen posture, nudged him with his foot, he was startled to note a pool of blood. Charcoal had slashed his wrists with an awl.

His wounds were quickly tended to, with flour to stop the bleeding, and sacking for bandage, then he was turned over to the police. Tried first for the murder of Medicine Pipe Stem, he was acquitted for lack of evidence. It was an ironic touch, but, of course, immaterial. On the charge of murdering Sgt. Wilde, the evidence was overwhelming, the trial brief, and the sentence death.

Execution was set for the morning of February 10, 1897. While awaiting sentence, Charcoal had initially refused to eat and, not having fully recovered from his attempt at suicide, rapidly lost strength. A few days before he was to hang, he was photographed while sitting in a blanket-covered chair in the jailyard. Wearing buckskin jacket and striped trousers provided by the photographer, he was captured on glass plate for posterity; his handcuffed wrists hidden under a hat, his eyes refusing to look into the camera lens.

On February 10, when guards entered his cell to escort him to the scaffold, (which had been erected in a horse corral) they found him unable to walk. To expedite matters, he was strapped into a chair and, as he chanted his death-song, dropped through the trap.

Earlier, Sgt. Wilde had been interred in the Pincher Creek cemetery. During the funeral, which was attended by several Indian chiefs of the region, one of Wilde's dogs turned on the pallbearers when they approached the body. Snapping and snarling, the animal refused to allow anyone to move the coffin and had to be shot. Wilde's prized horse, recovered with Charcoal's capture, earned a posthumous honor for her master a year later, when it was sent to England as part of the NWMP

contingent attending Queen Victoria's Diamond Jubilee cele-
brations. Upon completion of the ceremonies, it was formally
presented to Wilde's former unit, the Life Guards.   •

10

SWIFT RUNNER

It takes all kinds, according to an old saying, to make a world. The record graphically indicates that it also takes all kinds to kill.

Certainly one of the least likely candidates for murder was the Indian known as Katist-chen, or Swift Runner. Big, shy and kind-hearted, he was admired by the children, and respected by the Catholic priests of the mission of St. Albert, who had taken him in. The children appreciated the hours he spent watching over, and playing with them. The priests did all in their power to make his stay at the mission, situated just north of Edmonton, as pleasant as possible. For Swift Runner had known tragedy such as would break most men; tragedy which, nightly, haunted the big Cree brave, disturbing his sleep and making him cry out aloud in his agony.

Swift Runner's ordeal had begun in the fall of 1878, within 10 miles of the mission, when, with his mother, brother, wife and six children, he had gone hunting in the Sturgeon River area. But, instead of passing the winter as usual, with a plentiful supply of game, the family found themselves faced with starvation as Swift Runner and his brother failed to catch any game at all, either with rifle or trap. Within two months they were starving, and so weakened by hunger that all retreated to their blankets, where the adults enticed squirrels and rodents with the few crumbs of food they had left. Then even this small

source of meat was denied them and, in desperation, and with
the last of their strength, Swift Runner and the others had
turned to their teepee: shredding the rawhide with knives, then
boiling it into a thick, chewy mess that had the consistency—
and taste—of moccasins.

For some, this last resort was either too late or too little.
First to die was Swift Runner's youngest child, whom, he said,
he had buried in the trees. Then his mother and brother,
despairing, left camp to fend for themselves and did not return.
Soon, of the 10 youngsters and adults who had gone hunting
along the Sturgeon, only Swift Runner remained; his grief-
stricken wife having ended her misery with his rifle when the
last of their children died.

Only then had Swift Runner tried hiking in search of help.
Thus, in March of 1879, his appearance at St. Albert, where he
told his horrified hosts of the disaster that had befallen every
member of his family. It sounded almost too terrible to be true,
but the fathers, after questioning the big brave, urged him to
remain with them at the mission.

Two months passed, with the hulking 200-pounder easily
fitting into the mission routine. For all of his size, Swift Runner
soon showed himself to be a gentle giant; fond of the Indian
children who attended school there, and liked in return.

And that—but for the nightmares which tormented the Cree
when he tried to sleep—would have been the end of the
tragedy, had not one priest become increasingly suspicious of
his story.

From the beginning, Father Kemus had been unable to shake
the nagging feeling that something was not quite right with
Swift Runner's tale of horror. Although he could not possibly
deny the torment that the Indian endured nightly, Father
Kemus could not help but wonder if Swift Runner's nightmares
were those of a man bedevilled by grief, or by guilt. Were they
not, he wondered, the hell-fires of the damned?

The past winter, as those at the mission well knew, had not
been unusually severe, and none of the other Indians living in
the region had reported experiencing difficulty in finding
game. Neither of these facts made Swift Runner a liar,
yet...there was something about the man that the priest just
could not shake off. Was it, perhaps, the fact that, upon his
arrival at the mission, the huge Indian had not shown the
slightest indication of starvation? Rather, his frame had been
well-filled; an odd condition for a tall, 200-pound man to be in
after a months-long fight with starvation.

Despite these doubts, Father Kemus had remained silent. It
was not until Swift Runner suggested taking several of the

Indian youngsters on a hunting trip that the priest's suspicions suddenly gave way to panic. Although he knew he had absolutely nothing but the most circumstantial of evidence— more a sense of foreboding than anything else—he felt he must act. After stalling Swift Runner, he hastened to Fort Saskatchewan, and enlisted the aid of the NWMP.

Sub-Insp. Severe Gagnon listened patiently to the priest's impassioned charges, then, much to his caller's relief, instructed Sgt. Richard Steele and a half-breed interpreter named Brazeau to accompany Father Kemus back to St. Albert. Although the priest had had no more to go on than intuition, the veteran police officer believed where there is smoke there is fire, and felt there was nothing to be lost in at least questioning the man.

As instructed, Sgt. Steele interrogated the Cree. Swift Runner's account of the deaths of his entire family was so rambling and disjointed that, as much in frustration as in suspicion of foul play, Steele decided to escort him back to Fort Saskatchewan, where Insp. Gagnon would question him further.

At the police post, Swift Runner stuck to his story: the children had died of starvation, his mother and brother had wandered off, his wife had shot herself.

As he interrogated the Cree, Gagnon tried to pin him down on the finer details; at the same time, trying to decide whether Swift Runner was as slow-witted as he appeared to be, or if his dull appearance was a facade. For that matter, he had to concede, Swift Runner might well be intelligent, and telling the truth; his sometime irrational account of the loss of his family the natural result of the nightmare he had endured.

When further questioning left him more mystified than ever, Gagnon decided that the only possible way to decide the matter was to visit the death scene and, a week after Swift Runner was arrested, he was ordered to lead the police to the camp. Almost immediately, a drastic change occurred in the Cree's behavior. Despite his arrest, he had remained in good spirits, and had genially, if confusedly, answered all questions put to him. But, upon being instructed to lead Gagnon and company to the camp where his family died, Swift Runner became surly. Although he agreed to guide the police towards the Sturgeon River, Gagnon quickly came to the conclusion that he was, in fact, leading them in a circle. When he twice tried to escape during nights on the trail, Gagnon had him placed under close guard.

As Swift Runner became less cooperative and more withdrawn, Gagnon pondered his next move. It was a big country and, without the prisoner's help, they could waste a lot of time and still not find the ill-starred camp. The answer was provided by interpreter Brazeau, who calmly boiled a pot of tea, laced it with chewing tobacco, and let the evil concoction steep overnight. In the morning, the tar-like brew was given to Swift Runner, who not only accepted it, but drank it with relish. Then, instead of expiring on the spot, he mellowed, and, with his friendliness of old, promised to lead them right to the camp.

Shortly after, they came to a small lake, and Swift Runner motioned to an islet in its centre. Once on the island, the police proceeded through dense trees and undergrowth to a clearing. They did not have to look hard for evidences of the tragedy which had befallen Swift Runner's family. Everywhere, were the signs of death. The clearing was virtually littered with human remains. Here, a skull; there a piece of bone, skin or scalp.

At first glance, all was as Swift Runner had said it would be: the remains scattered about by wild animals. But discrepancies in his story showed immediately. Firstly, he had said that his mother and brother had left the camp. Yet there were eight skulls on the ground, not seven. Secondly, he had told how the starving family had cut the teepee into strips and boiled the rawhide for food. Yet there was the tent, cached in a spruce tree some distance from the camp.

But the most damning piece of evidence was a child's pair of stockings. In themselves they meant nothing, but, to a horrified Insp. Gagnon, they spelled murder. For if, in fact, wild animals had attacked the remains of the starvation victims, how could the stockings have found their way into an eye socket of what was obviously a baby's skull? The answer, of course, was that they had been placed their by human hands—if the hands of such a monster could be called human.

Returned to Fort Saskatchewan and formally charged with the murders of his mother, brother, wife and six children, Swift Runner appeared before Stipendiary Magistrate Hugh Richardson and a jury of six men in mid-August. The evidence against him was damning. One of the finer points that made his guilt undeniable was his cooking pot, which had been recovered from its hiding place on the lakeshore. Instead of being clean, as would be the case had its owners died of starvation, its inner walls were liberally coated with fat. Had the technology been available to the crown, it likely would have been shown that the fat was human.

Whatever, there was no use in pretending further and Swift Runner, who had maintained his stoicism throughout his two-

OUTLAWS
OF WESTERN CANADA

PHOTO SECTION

$11,500.00
REWARD

The Canadian Pacific Railway Coy.

offers a reward of $5,000 (Five Thousand Dollars) for the capture, dead or alive, of the three robbers who held up train 97 between Ducks and Kamloops on the morning of the 9th inst., or $1,000 (One Thousand Dollars) for the capture, dead or alive, of any one of the robbers.

The Dominion Government

Also offers $5,000 (Five Thousand Dollars) on the same terms as the above.

The Provincial Government

Offers One Thousand Five Hundred Dollars (Five Hundred Dollars for each man) for capture and conviction.

DESCRIPTION.

LEADER: About 5 ft. 7 in. in height, slim build, about 50 years of age, wore a grey stubby moustache, face and hands very much sun burnt, eyes somewhat inflamed, wore glasses, tattoo mark on back of right hand, wore a black slouch hat and a blue-black overcoat.

SECOND MAN: About 5 ft. 7 in. in height, medium build, weight about 170 lbs, black hair, dark complexion, very clear and distinct voice, with slight Cockney accent, wore an old blue sweater.

THIRD MAN: Age about 40 years, about 5 ft. 10 in. in height, light or reddish moustache and thin face.

By Order.

Kamloops, B. C., May 12th, 1906.

1

2

(1) *The dead or alive wanted poster issued for Bill Miner and his partners after the robbery of old '97, May 9, 1906. (2) The old Grey Fox himself, Bill Miner, as photographed upon his capture at Kamloops. (3) The Big Rock, now known as Bill Miner Rock, where the mail car was cut off the Imperial Limited.*

3

(1) Shorty Dunn, Bill Miner's accomplice, in 1906.
(2) The lawmen who brought the legendary Bill Miner to bay on the road at Murray Creek, 1906.
(3) Arrival of Bill Miner and company at the Kamloops provincial jail.
(4) Bill Miner's preliminary trial underway in the old Kamloops courtroom before Mayor Gordon, with Attorney-General Fulton acting as prosecuting attorney.

(1) *One of the worst atrocities of the Civil War was Quantrill's raid on Lawrence, Kansas, when 150 men, women and children were massacred.*
(2) *William Clarke Quantrill, the notorious guerilla leader who was fatally wounded in action in the closing hours of the Civil War.*
(3) *These miners had passed the hat to help pay the ailing Roderick's passage back to Seattle.*

1

2

3

(Above) Lumbering operations in Camp McKinney, in later years before the town was levelled by fire.

(Below) Richest producer in Camp McKinney was the Waterloo Shaft of the Cariboo Mine. The gold bars stolen by Roderick were mined here.

(Left) Supt. of Police Fred Hussey clinched the case against Jack Rowlands, "King Midas" of Scottie Creek.

(Below) Stage preparing to leave for the Cariboo from Barnard's Express office in Yale. It was a stage such as this that Jack Rowlands robbed of its shipment of gold bars and dust.

Entrance to Victoria Harbor during Ah-Chee-Wun's reign of terror.

Victoria's police barracks, where Ah-Chee-Wun was hanged.

(Above left) Moses Paul—he sparked the chain of events which ultimately claimed five lives. (Above right) Paul Spintlum—he smuggled a file into the jail, enabling his friend to escape.

A main street in Clinton, B.C., around 1900. This small town became the focal point of activity when Moses Paul and Paul Spintlum, Indian outlaws, were at large.

Wild Horse Creek, the gold camp for which "One-Ear" Charlie Brown headed upon his escape from Victoria.

(Opposite page) Almighty Voice, taken c. 1894, before he became an outlaw. (Above) The jail from which Almighty Voice escaped in 1895. This building still stands in Duck Lake. (Below) Site where Almighty Voice shot and killed Sgt. Colebrook.

ALMIGHTY VOICE

TAKEN INTO CUSTODY AT DUCK LAKE
ON A CHARGE OF KILLING CATTLE,
ALMIGHTY VOICE ESCAPED ON THE
NIGHT OF OCTOBER 22, 1895. HERE,
ONE WEEK LATER, HE SHOT AND
KILLED SERGEANT C.C. COLEBROOK,
N.W.M.P., WHO PURSUED HIM. IT
WAS NOT UNTIL MAY 28, 1897, THAT
THE FUGITIVE AND TWO INDIAN
COMPANIONS WERE SURROUNDED
BY MOUNTED POLICE AND CIVILIAN
VOLUNTEERS IN THE MINNICHINAS
HILLS. IN THE ENSUING TWO-DAY
ENGAGEMENT THE THREE INDIANS,
TWO POLICEMEN AND ONE CIVILIAN
WERE KILLED, AND THREE OTHERS
WOUNDED.

DEPARTMENT OF NATURAL RESOURCES

(1) Napoleon Venne, who aided the Mounted Police and was shot in the shoulder.
(2) Ernest Gundy, Duck Lake postmaster, killed in trying to rout Almighty Voice from the bluff.
(3) Graves of Almighty Voice's police victims in St. Mary's Church cemetery near Prince Albert. Left grave with cross — Cpl. Hockin; centre grave with tall stone marker — Sgt. Colebrook; right grave with cross — Const. Kerr.
(4) Mounties guarding the Minnichinas Hills where Almighty Voice and his two allies had taken refuge.

3

(1) The skeletal remains of Cree Indians, victims of Cree cannibal, Swift Runner.
(2) The monster, Swift Runner, in irons, has his picture taken with a Mounted Policeman, not shown.

(3) This famous picture of the Indian outlaw, Charcoal, was taken at Fort McLeod just a few days before his execution. The clothes were provided by Steele, the photographer, with the large hat serving to conceal the condemned man's handcuffs. Too feeble to stand, he was hanged sitting in a chair.

(1) Boone Helm, killer-cannibal of the western United States and Canada.

(2) Victoria Magistrate Augustus Pemberton, who gave Boone Helm a hefty jail sentence to allow extradition proceedings to begin.

(3) Legendary Indian outlaw Simon Gun-an-Noot, who defied police for 13 years and was acquitted of two murders for which he had been sought.

(4) Famous B.C. lawyer Stuart Henderson, who defended Simon Gun-an-Noot and won his acquittal.

Simon Gun-an-Noot's grave on the shore of Bowser Lake.

(Left) Henry Wagner — "The Flying Dutchman."

(Below) The Fraser and Bishop store, Union Bay, as it appeared the night of the Flying Dutchman's second raid. Constables Westaway and Ross, upon spotting a light in the store, entered from the post office on the left.

ALLEN McLEAN
Oldest, and leader of gang.

CHARLEY McLEAN
Middle brother.

(Below) Donald McLean, chief factor of Hudson's Bay Company, and father of infamous brothers.

ARCHIE McLEAN
Youngest of three brothers.

ALEXANDER HARE
Friend to evil McLeans.

Deserted cabin on Douglas Lake where the "Wild McLeans" were besieged and captured.

OUTLAWS

OF THE CANADIAN FRONTIER

T. W. PATERSON

This painting, commissioned for the cover of Outlaws of the Canadian Frontier, now out of print, depicts the scene where Bulldog Kelly lay in ambush for the unwary men. (Insert) Manvel Drainard — he survived the deadly ambush.

and-a-half-month-long imprisonment, took the witness stand and garrulously confessed to the murders of his wife and five of the children. The sixth, he stoutly maintained, had actually succumbed of starvation. He also continued to assert that his mother and brother had left the camp voluntarily; failing to account for the fact that eight, not seven, skulls were recovered from the death camp.

The verdict was inevitable and swift. Twenty minutes after they retired, the jurymen pronounced Swift Runner to be guilty as charged on eight counts of murder (having accepted that the owner of the missing skull had also been killed). The sentence of death was equally inevitable, Swift Runner being returned to the custody of the NWMP until Dec. 20, 1879, when he would pay the supreme penalty.

The four months remaining to Swift Runner were an eternity. For the nightmares that had haunted him, and which had helped to arouse the suspicious of Father Kemus, continued to make his life a misery. By day, he was not only good-natured, but seemingly unconcerned with his fate; by night, he was a man tormented almost beyond endurance by "bad spirits." Ironically, his spiritual advisor during the first months of his wait was Father Kemus, the man who had become convinced that within the grinning, shambling giant had lurked something unholy.

It remained for Father Leduc, Father Kemus' superior, to bring spiritual comfort to Swift Runner. Upon his return from Paris, Leduc had assumed charge of the prisoner, and succeeded in making him a Catholic. For days, he tried to convince the murderer that, in order to enjoy peace of mind, he must make peace with himself by complete confession. When, at last, Swift Runner did tell all—three days before execution—his was a story that sent shivers down his listeners' backs.

The family hunting expedition, he said, had begun as he had explained. At first, hunting had been successful and there was plenty to eat, Swift Runner managing to shoot several moose and bear. But, about the middle of February, Swift Runner had taken ill. Worse, their game supply dwindled, and the others were unable to keep them provisioned, when they had been forced to kill the dogs.

Swift Runner, by this time, had recovered somewhat and hiked to a Hudson's Bay Co. trading post on the Athabasca River, where, with the little money he had, he had bought some supplies and returned to the others. But these did not last long and, once again, they were faced with starvation. In desperation, his brother and mother had decided to go hunting

(Swift Runner remained firm on this point) and left the camp. Swift Runner remained with his wife, three sons and three daughters, as "starvation became worse and worse.

"For many days," he recounted, "we had nothing to eat. I advised my wife to start with the children and follow on the snow the tracks of my mother and brother, who perhaps had been lucky enough to kill a moose or a bear since they left us. For my part, though weak, I hoped that remaining alone I could support my life with my gun. All of my family left me with the exception of a little boy, 10 years of age."

For days, Swift Runner and his son remained in camp, growing steadily weaker. One morning, upon arising early, "an abominable thought" flashed across his mind.

"My son was lying down close to the fire, fast asleep. Pushed by evil spirits, I took my poor gun and shot him. The ball entered the top of his skull. Still he breathed. I began to cry, but what was the use. I then took my knife and sunk it twice into his side. Alas, he still breathed and I picked up a stick and killed him with it. I then satisfied my hunger by eating some of his flesh and lived on that for some days, extracting even the marrow from the bones."

Strength somewhat restored, Swift Runner then spent several days wandering through the woods, until he ran into his wife and children. His wife informed him that they had not found the others, and Swift Runner surmised that they must be dead. When he told his wife that their young son was also dead of starvation, he "noticed immediately (in the words of his interrogators) that they suspected the frightening reality."

Three days after he rejoined his family, his eldest son died and was buried after Swift Runner dug a grave with his axe. Then all were reduced to boiling leather strips from the tent, their shoes and buffalo robes.

As their ordeal worsened, Swift Runner became increasingly aware of the fact that his wife and surviving children were afraid of him; afraid of meeting the same fate as the youngest boy. He knew, he said, that they were plotting to flee.

"One morning I got up early, and I don't know why—I was mad. It seems to me that all the devils had entered my heart, My wife and children were asleep around me. Pushed by the evil spirit, I took my gun, and placing the muzzle against her, shot her. I then without delay took my hatchet and massacred my three little girls. There was now but only little boy, seven years old, surviving. I awoke him and told him to melt some snow for water at once. The poor child was so weakened by long fasting to make any reflection of the frightful spectacle under his eyes (these can only be the words of one of those taking down Swift Runner's confession).

"I took the bodies of my little girls and cut them up. I did the same with the corpse of my wife. I broke the skulls and took out the brains and broke up the bones in order to get the marrow. My little son and I lived for seven or eight days on the flesh—I eating the flesh of my wife and children, he the flesh of his mother and sisters."

By the time Swift Runner and his son had consumed the others, it was spring, and he broke camp. Migrating ducks were landing on the lake, and he could bag sufficient game. But he was afraid to meet people; telling the boy that they would soon encounter others, who would soon know the truth and demand Swift Runner's life. "As to you," he told the lad, "there is no fear; say all you know; no harm will be done to you."

One day near Egg Lake, after a successful duck hunt, Swift Runner began to brood. He had relatives nearby and, faced with the knowledge that his terrible crime must soon be revealed, he was again seized by "the devil." As he sat beside the fire, he ordered his son to "go and fetch something five or six paces off... In order to live longer far from people, and to put out of the way the only witness to my crimes, I seized my gun and killed the last of my children and ate him as I did the others."

It is interesting to note that, even in his confession (which, according to those attending him during his final hours, did bring him peace of mind) Swift Runner denied having slain his mother and brother; insisting that they had perished after going off. However, in other conversations with officials, he had admitted to having killed and eaten both. Thus the eight skulls recovered from the cannibal's camp had been those of his mother, brother, wife, three daughters and two of his sons. That of the last youngster, whom he had killed at another site, was not recovered.

Swift Runner waited for death without fear, his sleep no longer disturbed by bad spirits, as the final arrangements were made for his execution. As Sheriff Richards, who was to officiate, proceeded from Battleford, a scaffold was erected. Despite the length of his overland journey to Fort Saskatchewan, Richards arrived there on the evening of December 19, and read a beaming and unconcerned Swift Runner the death warrant. Early the next morning, with the mercury hovering at -40 degrees, a last-minute hitch developed when no volunteers for conducting the execution were forthcoming. Sheriff Richards was about to handle the grim chore personally, when a former soldier named Rogers stepped forward, and Swift Runner was conducted from his cell to the

scaffold, which had been erected in the wintry yard adjacent
to the guardroom.

Escorted by Sheriff Richards, Insp. William Jarvis, policemen, and the faithful Father Leduc, Swift Runner approached
the gallows. Rather than being daunted by its appearance, he
seemed to be intrigued by its construction. Immediately upon
being led up the steps, his arms and legs were pinioned. Before
the hood was put in place, the mass murderer confessed his
guilt, and thanked his captors for their kind treatment, Father
Leduc for his ministrations, then, with a shiver, jokingly
mocked his executioner for making him wait.

His wait was brief. A split second later, to the mournful
wailing of the Indians among the crowd of 50 spectators, Swift
Runner plunged through the trap. Not only had he made
criminal history by claiming the most victims in Saskatchewan
history, but his had been the first capital trial by jury in the
so-called North West Territories, and his execution was the
first conducted by the NWMP.

It was also, in the words of an experienced eyewitness, the
prettiest hanging he had ever seen.   •

11

BOONE HELM

Soldier, sailor, saint and sinner; the famous, the forgotten; pioneer Victoria knew them all. But of the many colorful characters who have enacted their roles, large and small, on the provincial stage, there is one without peer. A monster in human guise who left a bloody trail of murder and violence— including the ultimate iniquity of cannibalism—from Missouri to British Columbia.

As final insurance against being forgotten, infamous Boone Helm left us another legacy: A tantalizing tale of lost treasure. Still hidden in the Cariboo, at the foot of an ancient cedar, is $32,000 in raw gold, ill-earned fruit of a triple slaying.

On that fateful afternoon of more than a century ago, when Helm swaggered up busy Wharf Street to give his black career international status, his evil reputation had preceded him. A "dangerous and bad character," said the *Colonist* with admirable restraint. Just how dangerous and how bad is readily apparent from the briefest glance at his record.

Born in Kentucky about 1828, Boone came from an ill-starred family, all five brothers dying violently. If the other Helms were anything like slack-jawed Boone, their early exits were nowhere near being early enough!

Tall and powerful, skilled with gun, knife and horse, Boone's extra-curricular activities began in Monroe County, Missouri. Given to uncontrollable rages which hinted of deeper

93

emotional problems, 20-year-old Boone did make a stab at respectability of sorts, marrying a girl of good repute. The shaky alliance even saw a visit by the stork, but by then Mrs. Helm had realized her colossal error, securing a divorce soon after her daughter was born.

Footlose and fancy free again, Boone decided to try greener fields. Texas beckoned, so he asked his friend, Littlebury Shoot, to throw in. Shoot was all for heading west, except he'd heard California was the place to go. The friends continued to tout Texas and California respectively. Came the day of departure, they still had not agreed. On Littlebury's front porch, Boone declared that, after due consideration, it had to be Texas or else.

"Or else what?" asked not-too-bright but firm Littlebury. Boone's reply was sharp and to the point. He dissolved the brief partnership with his bowie knife, poor Littlebury dying without a sound.

Since Shoot was Helm's one and only friend, this should give some idea as to how the lanky Kentuckian treated strangers!

In all due fairness, it should be pointed out that, in wilder moments, Boone could display a certain degree of bravado. Not bravery, mind you, but bravado. Like the time he'd been told the sheriff was looking for him. With all the courage a jug of rotgut could render, he had charged into the courthouse to profanely demand what the so-and-so sheriff wanted of him—forgetting, in his righteous indignation, to check his horse at the door.

But there were those who thought dimly of Helm's unbecoming behaviour, particularly as far as Littlebury Shoot was concerned, and galloped in pursuit, running him to earth on an Indian reserve. If ever a case of lynch law was justified, this was it. Sadly, the Missourians turned him over to the authorities, with the result that Boone found himself convicted of murder and sentenced to an asylum. His manner was not only unbecoming, ruled the court, but unbalanced.

Now, for the first time in his unholy life, Helm displayed complete self control. Polite, penitent, he was the prize patient. Popular with staff and guards, he soon was allowed freedom of the grounds under supervision, until there finally came a day when his guard wasn't watching and Boone slipped into a grove of willows and out of the state.

When next we hear of our hero, he is in California. Maybe he concluded old Littlebury Shoot had known what he was talking about, after all. Whatever, wild as was California in 1858, it wasn't wild enough to tolerate Helm. Several shootings later, he was on the run again, this time to Oregon. There, he learned sunny California was so upset at losing such a leading citizen that it was signing extradition papers. Boone decided that it was high time he went underground. Which he promptly did— almost permanently.

While at The Dalles, he heard that a party was setting out for Camp Floyd, Utah, 60 miles southwest of Salt Lake City. The expedition had not been on the trail long when its newest member, a tall, foul-mouthed Southerner, had a brainwave: Why travel 500 miles to Camp Floyd when they could steal the Walla Walla tribe's 2,000 horses? His adventurous companions fell in with the scheme and it might have worked but for Dr. William Groves, who secretly resigned from the party then warned the Indians.

The disappointed six resumed their expedition, reaching Raft River without incident, where they were attacked by Digger Indians. The brief battle ended without casualty but, at Bannack River, the warriors raided camp under cover of darkness, killing the sentry. When the five survivors made wicked Wasatch Mountain Range, they faced a much more lethal foe: Winter.

Blizzards and sub-zero temperatures dogged the struggling party, until they finally sought refuge in an abandoned cabin. They could go no farther. Killing the exhausted horses one by one, they existed on the smoked meat and rested. After regaining their strength, they invested the time in making crude snowshoes of horsehide. When the weather cleared, they resumed their journey on foot, only to be caught in another blizzard and soon all were exhausted, almost frozen.

Unable to continue, three of the party decided to make shelter and wait out the storm, Helm and Elijah Burton electing to proceed. None of the three was ever seen again.

Weeks later, a gaunt Helm, dressed in buckskin, and an Indian visited the camp of fur buyer John W. Powell. The blood-chilling tale Helm then told his shocked host made his name among the most infamous of American history.

He and Burton, he told Powell, had stumbled upon another deserted cabin soon after leaving their comrades. Both were starving but Burton could not take another step. With the last of his strength, Helm had staggered on to Cantonement Loring, only to find the post deserted, the food gone. He then returned to Burton to find his comrade dead. Helm said Burton had shot himself, thinking Helm would not return. (Historians consider it more likely that Helm shot Burton).

Then, continued the monster in buckskins without batting an eye, he had butchered and dressed his partner like a steer, and proceeded to consume Burton over the next few days.

Partially recuperated, he wrapped the remainder of his larder, a leg, in a blanket and headed for Camp Floyd. Sadly, he came across the camp of an Indian who guided him to Powell's camp and rescue.

Accompanying the trader to Salt Lake City, Helm turned to his horse stealing. Also, according to the record, renting his gun to the dreaded Danites, the Mormon secret police. After two known murders, he drifted on, through California and back to Oregon. "Several" further killings were added to his record in this period.

Then it was across the line to Idaho, operating out of the mining camp of Florence, until he gunned down an unarmed gambler named Dutch Fred. Once again he was on the run, word of his latest atrocity sweeping the Northwest.

This, then, is the sterling character who sauntered off a small steamer onto Enterprise Wharf, Oct. 12, 1862. Having exhausted his luck in every western American state and territory, Helm had resolved to try Victoria. Hours later, he was grimly surveying a tiny cell in Bastion Square's police barracks. A strange welcome indeed for such an exemplary traveller. For, being a stranger to our cruel shores and cold customs, how was he to know he was expected to pay for his fruit and drinks?

Three days later, the *Colonist* reported: "Boone Helm—This man, who, it is alleged, bears a horrible reputation in California and other localities on the Pacific Coast, was brought before the police magistrate yesterday on a remand from Monday last.

"The prisoner (who is not a bad looking man) was defended by Mr. Bishop, by whom it was urged that a prejudice had been created against him in the minds of residents, and that a subscription had been taken up to defray the cost of prosecution. The police officers present denied that any such arrangements existed so far as they were aware, and the chief of police swore that he was known as a bad character.

"The proprietor of the Adelphi Saloon testified that he had procured drinks there, and that when pay was requested, replied: 'Don't you know that I'm a desperate character?' Sgt. Blake said that people who knew the accused best were afraid of him. The magistrate ordered Helm to find security to be of good behaviour for the term of six months, himself in 50 pounds sterling, and two securities in 20 pounds each; in default, to suffer one month's imprisonment."

Which would indicate Victorians had Helm's number!

The real reason for the hefty sentence was to hold the penniless outlaw where he could do no harm until word was telegraphed to the Florence sheriff. Unfortunately, that Idaho worthy must have been busy, as, when finally extradition papers arrived, Helm's month had expired. Outraged at Victoria's inhospitable ways, he had caught the first mainland steamer, heading for the easier manner of boomtown Fort Yale.

Alas, the Cariboo was no kinder to the destitute newcomer, particularly when he took steps to better his financial standing. Thirty years after, pioneer A. Browning recalled his brief but unpleasant encounter with Mr. Helm.

On his way to the gold fields, Browning "met shoals of men returning from the mines. Some were dead-broke prospectors, others disappointed gamblers, and not a few who were ready for any dare-devilism that would bring good pay.

"The trail leading down the mountain to the Forks of Quesnelle was a mile long, and as I came near the base of the mountain I saw on the trail on the other side of the little village, a procession of men carrying three stretchers. I found on meeting them that they were carrying three dead men. They were found on the trail coming from Cariboo, robbed and murdered, for it was known that each of them was carrying bags of gold dust from Williams Creek to the coast.

"Who was the murderer, or who were the murderers? Everybody said in whispers it was Boone Helm, a gambler and cutthroat who had escaped from the San Francisco Vigilante Committee. He was known to have been on the trail and he it was I probably met a few hours after the murder was committed."

As the only constable was drunk, "and if he had been sober was of no use in an emergency like this," Mr. Browning was elected coroner at a mass meeting of enranged miners. After a verdict of wilful murder had been returned, the miners elected him magistrate, complete with a "young Jew as magistrate's clerk." The court was formally constituted, and one or two suspicious men arrested, examined, and then let go, for everybody said the murderer was Boone Helm.

"Pursuit down the trail was determined on, and $700 raised to pay the cost of pursuers. Boone, I imagine, got wind of all this, and escaped across the line and when afterwards we heard he was hung to a limb of a tree for horse stealing we thought the murders of Quesnelle were avenged."

At least one other had had the misfortune of meeting Helm on the lonely trail before he retreated across the line. W.T. Collinson and "Irish" Tommy Harvey had travelled with the murdered trio, a miner named Sokoloski and two unnamed Frenchmen from Antler Creek as far as Keithley Creek, where

the ill-fated trio paused for dinner, Collinson and Harvey
continuing. They reached Quesnel Forks that evening where,
the next afternoon, they saw their three late companions
carried into town.

"They had made a brave fight," Collinson recounted, "every
man's pistol (good six shooters) was empty, and each man had
a bullet through his head. Boone Helm and his chum killed
these three men, took and hid the dust and if no stranger has
found it it is there yet, for Boone left the country."

As "proof of that," Collinson recalled his own encounter
with the Kentucky killer a few days later. "I met Boone Helm
and his chum at Little Bloody Run, just below Cap Venable's, a
few miles above Cooke & Kimble's ferry, now Spence's bridge.
The first thing I heard was, 'Throw up your hands', and looking
up I saw the muzzle of a double-barrelled shotgun about four
feet from my head."

At the other end of the small cannon was dear Mr. Helm,
who glowered menacingly at Collinson during the five minutes
or so it took his partner to slash open the traveller's
saddlebags and search his pockets. For their trouble, they
received three Mexican dollars and three British shillings,
overlooking Collinson's pouch of dust which was rolled up in an
old shirt. Returning his emptied revolver, they "told me to git
and not look back. As my road was downhill I lost no time!"

The next time Collinson saw the outlaw, "was at Sumas in
the spring of 1864, I think. He was along with a pack train...on
his way to get the dust hid at Quesnelle and next day I got on
my way to intercept Helm at Yale, but the marshall from Port
Townsend was there and took him...on a charge of murder."

Once again Helm took his leisure in a Bastion Square cell,
until hustled over the line in irons, to make his inglorious exit
from the B.C. stage. Returned to Idaho, he was soon,
remarkably, at liberty. Older brother Tex, it seems, was a man
of influence, not to mention money. At the brief trial,
once-valuable witnesses were amazingly mute; Boone Helm
was a free man.

But—finally—the end of his bloody trail was near. Months
later, Virginia City vigilantes exterminated the notorious
Henry Plummer gang through generous doses of lead and
hemp. On a warm January day, 1864, as 6,000 watched in grim
satisfaction, five of the gang plunged to eternity from five
packing cases. Overhead, the roof-beam of an unfinished cabin
jerked spasmodically at the sudden weight, then was still.
Among the hated five was that "savage, reckless, defiant
marauder of the goldrush days at Cariboo; robber, assassin,
and reputed cannibal"—Boone Helm.

Today, "beside a lonely, partially overgrown trail heading out from the Cariboo ghost town of Quesnel Forks to the scant remains of another town of the past, Antler Creek, there stands a particular cedar tree." Here, in the forest monarch's trailing roots, according to popular legend, are the rotted saddlebags of poor Sokoloski and the two Frenchmen— containing an estimated $32,000 in raw gold. Pioneers were convinced that Helm murdered his partner then hid the gold in case he was arrested. Helm knew he was wanted for the murders, yet, as Collinson reported, he dared to return to the area less than a year later, to be arrested and extradited to Idaho.

If the gold is there today, it is the last remaining link with Boone Helm, cannibal-murderer of the Cariboo.   •

12

SIMON GUN-AN-NOOT

Hidden in the isolated 9,000-foot Coast Mountains northeast of Stewart, British Columbia, is lonely Bowser Lake. It is here that is to be found the neglected resting place of B.C.'s most remarkable Indian.

Picket fence and wooden cross sagging drunkenly with age, and overgrown with bush, this is the grave of legendary Kispiox brave Simon Peter Gun-an-Noot. This amazing man is remembered throughout Western Canada as the fugitive who eluded the entire B.C. Provincial Police force for 13 exciting years—and when he finally surrendered, was acquitted of the murders for which he had been sought!

Gun-an-Noot was a giant in stature, strength and stamina. Born Zghun-min-hoot ("young bears that run up trees") on the Haguilite Reserve near Hazelton, the Wolf Clan brave stood over six feet in height and weighed 200 pounds of sinew and muscle. Famous for his marksmanship and hunting and trapping ability, he was known to travel up to 40 miles a day through the wildest terrain without tiring.

At an early age Simon was converted to Christianity, "in which he staunchly lived in word and deed." He was an amazing man in every respect. But from childhood, Gun-an-Noot seems to have been the victim of a curse; a curse that ultimately proved to be tragic prophecy...

The son of a notorious firebrand, Nazgh-guhn (commonly

known as Nah-Gun), Gun-an-Noot had two brothers and a
sister. When an uncle murdered a Sikanni Indian, the sister
was turned over to the injured tribe as payment, native law
stating "a life for a life." Several years later, Simon's brother
Dhin accidentally killed a playmate with the father's musket
and fled into the forest.

The dead boy's parents then demanded retribution. Nah-
Gun offered his every possession, including a prized hunting
ground—and Gun-an-Noot. Although they had the choice of
enslaving the lad or slaying him, the grieving parents refused
either. Agreeing to Nah-Gun's previous offers, they shunned
the youth superstitiously, muttering, "There is murder in his
blood." Instead, they accepted his height in blankets and he was
free.

But their damning words would haunt him for the rest of his
life.

The murders which made Gun-an-Noot a fugitive—and made
history—occurred in June, 1906. At that time he returned from
Victoria, the provincial capital, where he had made a large
sale on his winter's catch of furs.

One night Simon, his brother-in-law Peter Hi-ma-dan, and
several friends visited Two-Mile House. Although a light
drinker himself, he willingly treated his companions to round
after round, and the atmosphere rapidly grew louder and
happier.

But not all of those lining the crowded bar were Gun-an-
Noot's friends. An unsavory half-breed, Alec McIntosh,
watched him jealously. The cause of their feud has been lost to
history, but it is known McIntosh hated him with all his dark
soul. And the more he drank, the more reckless he became.

Finally he decided to goad the popular trapper into a fight
and beat him senseless, probably hoping this would shame him
in front of his comrades. It was a fatal decision.

Gun-an-Noot turned his broad back on the first insults, but
McIntosh soon pierced his armour. It was common knowledge
that Simon would not tolerate slurs directed at the lowest type
of woman. When the drunken 'breed began recounting his
exploits among local Indian women, Simon flushed with anger.

McIntosh seized his opportunity and bellowed, "The Kispiox
squaws are the easiest. I can have my way with any of them!"
and glared meaningfully at the trapper.

Eyes flashing, Gun-an-Noot strode toward his antagonist and
demanded, "My wife, too?"

"Specially your—"

Before McIntosh could finish the lie, Simon's mighty fist
buried itself in his face, spinning him to the floor.

When police later investigated, all they could learn was that Simon gave McIntosh a well-earned thrashing, as the others dazedly watched. Most of the witnesses agreed, however, that when Simon left, he swore, "I'll get my rifle and rid the world of this beast!"

Brother-in-law Peter Hi-ma-dan wanted to shoot McIntosh on the spot.

That ended the party and McIntosh then departed, it being four o'clock in the morning.

Hours later, Constable James Kirby was examining a bullet-ridden body on the trail near Two-Mile Creek. It was Alec McIntosh. He had been shot in the heart—"while riding a galloping horse." Whoever killed him had been an extraordinary marksman.

As Constable Kirby began packing the corpse into Hazelton, he was informed that another body had been found, a quiet rancher named Max LeClair. Like McIntosh, he, too had been shot from his horse. Again, the mysterious rifleman had struck the heart. "The paths of the bullets did not vary by so much as a fraction of an inch." Kirby surmised the killer had knelt beside the trail and waited until his victims had passed.

The constable began tracing witnesses for the inquest. When he learned Gun-an-Noot and Hi-ma-dan had not been seen since the fatal morning, he swore in special constables and headed for Simon's home. There he found only Gun-an-Noot's wife Sarah. She was uncommunicative.

Checking the house and corrall, the posse discovered Simon had fled. Four horses had been slain to prevent the police using them. By the time of the inquest, Kirby's only success had been the arrest of Gun-an-Noot's father Nah-Gun for "acting suspiciously and aiding his son in flight."

The inquest, held on June 9, 1906, uncovered little. When the 13 witnesses had been heard, it was known only that Gun-an-Noot and McIntosh had fought. All the party-goers had been too drunk to remember details clearly. The jury returned the verdict, "We, having heard all the evidence relating to the above case, have come to the conclusion that Alec McIntosh was killed by a gunshot wound on the morning of the 19th inst. between Two-Mile Creek and the hospital, and are agreed that it was a case of wilful murder by a person of the name of Simon Peter Gun-an-Noot (Indian) of Kispiox village."

In the slaying of LeClair, the jury said it "strongly suspected" Peter Hi-ma-dan, and warrants were issued for the missing braves.

This probably is the only case in provincial history in which a coroner's jury literally convicted two men of murder—in absentia, without the accused having legal counsel, and with insufficient evidence. Nah-Gun had realized from the beginning that Simon stood little chance and urged him to run; the chase that would last 13 years and cost the nation more than $100,000 had begun...

From the very start police knew charging Gun-an-Noot with murder was one thing, capturing him another. He knew "every pass, creek and thicket for more than 200 miles back in the mountain fastnesses" and traversed country which veteran woodsman declared "impassable." To Simon, "the whole Omineca country...was an open book." This area is as large as France!

But when the first posse crossed the Kiskigas River, they had little difficulty picking up his and Peter's trail and soon found 14 of their dogs. Simon had tethered the animals where they would warn him of the officers' approach—and vanished.

As the weeks began to pass, the search was intensified. Weary men criss-crossed wicked mountain passes and raging rivers, fighting summer heat, mosquitoes, blackflies and exhaustion. Then winter brought biting frost, heavy snows and gales. But the determined hunters pressed on, checking every lead and rumor. The first year earned only frustration.

By now the entire country followed the case with interest, silently admiring the Indian who defied the greatest manhunt in Dominion history. A desperate government added fresh men to the search, offered $1,000 reward and brought in a Pinkerton detective at a cost of $11,000. The efforts netted absolutely nothing.

Time and again posses knew they had come close to the dusky phantom, only to lose him. They also knew he continually visited his family, slipping through the most elaborately planned cordons with ease. Always he brought them furs to buy supplies.

Then the fugitives' families slipped into the forest to join them, increasing their chances of capture. Yet Simon continued to elude the police, popping up here and there until the weary searchers thought they were hunting a will-o'-wisp. On at least one occasion, Simon actually slipped through a patrol to steal its cache of grub!

Dozens of experienced trackers and hunters joined the quest, hoping to earn the reward. None was successful.

Now Gun-an-Noot had inspired such admiration among the hardy settlers of B.C. that many refused to co-operate with police. And authorities grudgingly conceded that if Simon were the cold-blooded killer as charged, why had he not ambushed any of his pursuers? Every officer admitted he had had ample opportunity.

One of those hunting Simon was Constable Otway Wilkie. In his report, he briefly mentions one of the countless incidents that made life all the harder for the hunters.

"We constructed a raft to go down the lake and then put our effects on board and started, but had an accident, the raft running into a snag and throwing everything into the water. We recovered everything, but the rice, tea, and sugar were spoiled..."

Wilkie concluded his report, a chronicle of understated hardship and courage, with the following: "I received no definite information re: Gun-an-Noot or Peter Hi-ma-dan on my trip... In my opinion, owing to the difficulty of travelling in winter, a summer hunt would be better during July and August, as horses can travel on the trails then. Either that or give up the chase until some reliable information is obtained." He had covered 1,500 miles in this single expedition.

It was not until years later, when Simon surrendered, that Constable Wilkie learned he had come "closer to taking Gun-an-Noot than any other officer engaged in the search." And had not Simon stopped Peter Hi-ma-dan, the unsuspecting officer's reward would have been a bullet.

The fugitives, cold, exhausted and almost out of supplies, stumbled into Wilkie's party. Glimpsing the patrol ahead, they threw themselves into the snow and scrambled to cover—their tracks betraying them. They could not remain hidden but could not slip away unnoticed. It looked like the end of the trail.

Constable Wilkie, still unaware of their presence, advanced toward their refuge. He was almost upon them when, unaccountably, he retreated to his party and the Indians were saved.

The following day, Simon and Peter suffered the same unnerving experience. Once more Wilkie unwittingly approached their lair, a tiny cave. Once more he was framed in Peter's sights. Again Simon restrained his hotheaded comrade, reminding him that then they really would be murderers. Peter reluctantly lowered his rifle, and Wilkie returned to his men, never imagining just how near he had come to the long-sought outlaws—and death.

It was about this time that Nah-Gun escaped from the Hazelton jail, where he had been held since Gun-an-Noot's flight. Although a special guard had been hired to watch him, he succeeded in prying loose a board in the stockade outhouse and vanished into the mountains to join his son.

More years passed, World War I began, the fugitives still

continuing their lonely struggle. And still they were free. The intensive manhunt had dwindled in size and spirit. Officials had decided to wait until Simon blundered and walked into their hands.

Just before old Nah-Gun died, he asked Simon to bury him beneath the cottonwoods lining Bowser Lake. The grieving son nodded without hesitation, although he knew full well he would have to carry his father on his back, 40 miles through forest—and perhaps through police patrols—to the lake. Strapping the heavy body to a pack board, he began the two-day-long hike. Finally arriving at Bowser Lake, he buried his father with Christian rites, and erected a tiny wooden cross.

But the constant strain and hardships were proving too much for Peter Hi-ma-dan. Losing his temper, he accused Simon of causing the entire chain of tragedy and set out on his own. He intended to live with a tribe east of Stikine River, but found they knew his identity and shunned him for fear of government reprisal. Bitterly discouraged, he rejoined Simon. At one time it was rumored he had died.

Yet his loyalty to Simon (or his distrust of police) was such that, when informed by "moccasin telegraph" that he had unofficially been offered amnesty, he did not surrender.

According to one report, "Evidence, or lack of it, now appeared that made the pursuit of Peter seem a foolish venture. If he were caught there wasn't the slightest hint, or even rumor, to connect him with the killing of McIntosh and LeClair. In the first flush of excitement following the crime there had been wild rumors that Hi-ma-dan and not Gun-an-Noot, had done the shooting. These, however, had drifted into the limbo of forgotten things and nobody seemed to recall Hi-ma-dan being anywhere near the scene of the shooting.

"We know this to be wrong, but things being what they were it was decided to forget about Hi-ma-dan and concentrate on getting Gun-an-Noot. Besides, there was a chance that if Gun-an-Noot was alone he would be unable to evade capture for very long."

During the seventh year of exile, Simon and Peter ventured into the isolated Stikine River camp of R.T. Hankin. The Yukon Telegraph Line employee and two companions were warming themselves by their little fire when the Indians strode into the flickering light. With a start, Hankin recognized Gun-an-Noot but remained silent when he noticed the visitors had left their rifles on their dog sled.

The fugitives wolfed down the grub which their host offered. Then a grinning Simon amazed Hankin with a detailed account

of the latter's activities, indicating he "was aware of what was
going on for hundreds of miles around."

About one year later, Simon again appeared at one of
Hankin's camps, bringing along some caribou meat. After a
meal of bacon and beans, the two men talked far into the night.
Seeming to trust the linesman, Simon told of his lonely struggle,
of the agonies his family had suffered, ending with the hopeful
question, "What happen to me if I give up?"

Hankin was slow to answer, afraid of frightening Gun-an-
Noot by acting too anxiously. "...You will have a fair trial...the
court will see that you have a good lawyer..."

"No!" exclaimed the outlaw, rising to his feet, "I pay
everything myself! When I have $2,000 I come," and he
disappeared into the night.

But it was another Yukon Telegraph Line employee who
ultimately convinced Simon to give up. Like Hankin, George
Biernes encountered the fugitive deep in the wilderness when
Gun-an-Noot entered his camp. They met many times after
that, Biernes never missing an opportunity to encourage the
outlaw's surrender. Finally Simon agreed.

The best account of the saga's conclusion is that of late
provincial police Corporal Sperry Cline, a friend of Biernes,
who wrote:

"Biernes went to Victoria and saw Henderson (famous
criminal lawyer Stuart Henderson), who readily agreed to
defend Simon. He came to Hazelton where we had several
consultations. The question of financing the defence arose and
it was agreed that Biernes would collect the reward and give it
to Simon for his defence. Henderson then returned to Victoria
and waited for Biernes to contact Simon, which he did:

"The next spring Henderson came again to Hazelton, and he
and Biernes met Simon about a hundred miles up river from
Hazelton, and agreed, at Simon's request, to wait another year
in order that he might have next winter's trapping to raise the
amount required for the defence. Simon apparently could not
understand how Biernes could collect the reward when we
were not going to arrest him, but were allowing him to
surrender. He probably wanted more time to consider the
whole proposal..."

But now came an unexpected hitch. During all Henderson's
planning, he had overlooked one little point—"the laws
regarding counselling and comforting outlaws. One statute,
enacted about the Middle Ages, provided the most direful
punishment for such an offence." Henderson carefully warned
Biernes, Cline and Gun-an-Noot not to mention a word of their
strange conspiracy.

Corporal Cline goes on, "The following summer, Henderson returned to Hazelton, contacted Simon as before, and a date was set for Simon to come in and surrender. The date arrived and Simon did not appear. In a day or so we learned that he and his family were encamped several miles from Hazelton. His reason for not coming at the appointed hour was the fact his wife was expecting a visit from the stork, and he would not come until this event occurred.

"We waited for ten days. I went about my duties in a dither. I expected the fact of his being in the district would leak out and a cry go up for his arrest. But the baby arrived and Simon promised to come in two days later.

"Everything was set for his arrival. I had taken the precaution to have the jail empty, possibly by shutting my eyes to several minor offences," Cline continued. "The afternoon before he was to come in, I was standing in front of the police office, and saw Henderson approaching. I saw at once by his appearance that something had gone wrong. This was the only occasion on which I ever saw him agitated. As he came up he started to splutter. My heart went down to my boots. I thought that possibly Simon had been discovered by someone, and had done some more shooting.

"After Henderson had calmed himself somewhat, he shouted to me: "Get out of town. Get out of town. If Simon surrenders to you, you will have to give evidence regarding the surrender. Then you will be cross-examined on what happened before, and God knows what you will say!"

This posed a problem for Cline, as he could not leave his post unless relieved. Fate stepped in, however, in the form of a subpoena to give evidence in a case at Prince Rupert, and he was immediately relieved by Constable John Kelly.

"I met Kelly at the station, took him into my confidence," recounted Cline, "told him of Simon's intended surrender and took the same train for Prince Rupert. Kelly was an experienced constable with several years' service in the northern interior. He had heard all the rumors and stories concerning Simon, and when I told him what was happening I will never forget the look he gave me as much as to say: 'Do you expect me to believe that?' "

While in Prince Rupert, Corporal Cline was "on pins and needles" until he read newspaper headlines declaring "GUN-AN-NOOT SURRENDERED."

During the weeks required to gather witnesses for the preliminary hearing, Simon was held in Cline's Hazelton jail, where they "became well acquainted and a lasting friendship grew up between us."

"I soon learned that Simon, after his life of freedom in the wilds, was subject to claustrophobia and from then on, on receiving his word of honor, stopped locking the jail which was a great relief to him. This once caused me some embarrassment and led me to deceive him on the only occasion that I ever did so.

"Constable Kelly remained with me a few days after the surrender until headquarters was convinced that it did not require two constables to hold Simon. We both had been holding prisoners in our jails for years, and it had become second nature for us to lock all doors behind us on all occasions.

"One day, one of us (we never decided which) absent-mindedly, on coming out of the cell corridor, locked the door. I came in a short time later and noticed that the door was locked. I knew this could mean trouble and that I would have to find an explanation. The jail that we were occupying at that time was a large ramshackle affair which had been hastily thrown together during boom days. There was a door at the far end of the corridor which opened into a shed at the back. I hurried through the building and unlocked this door as quietly as possible and walked as unconcernedly as I could to where Simon was sitting.

"He was crouched like a caged beast ready to spring, eyes aflame and every muscle tensed. I realized that I had to do something and do it as quickly as I could. I turned my back to him and said: 'We are keeping the back door open now. Come and I will show you the way out. I guess that Mr. Kirby forgot to tell you.' He followed me into the yard where I left him to relax while I went home to sweat it out.

"I also, at his request, allowed him to work outside which seemed to surprise the people of Hazelton. One day a kind old lady, on passing my yard and seeing Simon behind me with an axe, ran for help, sure that I would be murdered by that awful Indian!"

Simon was committed to trial, which was held in Vancouver on a change of venue. The court proceedings, after thirteen exhausting years of flight, were anti-climactic. After hearing the brief and inconclusive evidence, the jury quickly returned a verdict of not guilty. On October 8, 1919, Simon walked through the streets a free man.

Several months later, Peter Hi-ma-dan surrendered to Corporal Cline and was discharged at the preliminary hearing. The greatest manhunt in Canadian history finally had ended...

Simon returned to his family and trapping. In 1933 he visited his father's grave at Bowser Lake. While there, he became ill and died shortly after. He was buried beside old Nah-Gun.

Today Simon Peter Gun-an-Noot's memory is very much alive. Each time storytellers relate the colorful legends of provincial heritage, his name is always mentioned. Time has failed to dim his exciting story...or solve the mystery that sent him fleeing into the wilderness.

Today the question remains: If Simon did not slay McIntosh and LeClair, who did? There are a number of theories.

During Simon's and Peter's exile, Mrs. Hi-ma-dan died at Hazelton. As she lay on her deathbed, she made a startling confession: She had killed Max LeClair. "On that night I went to Two-Mile to get Peter. On the way there I met LeClair on the trail. He talked for a little while and then said bad things to me and wanted me to do bad things with him..."

She resisted his forced advances, Mrs. Hi-ma-dan continued. Breaking free, she ran to her horse and grabbed a rifle from the saddle. Seeing this, LeClair quickly mounted his own pony and galloped off. The hysterical woman raised the rifle, fired and LeClair spun from the saddle.

"I was beside the trail crying, frightened at what I had done, when I heard another pony coming. It stopped and I looked up and saw Gun-an-Noot. He asked me why I was crying and I told him. He said for me to go home and forget it and he would tell people he had shot LeClair. He made me promise never to tell anybody. I went home. Gun-an-Noot took me there. He was going back to Two-Mile to kill McIntosh when his father came and said that McIntosh had been killed. His father said that everybody blamed him for shooting McIntosh."

The woman died moments after "confessing."

Few believed her story. She said she had been standing when she fired: evidence indicated the killer had been kneeling. And how could a distraught woman fire so accurately in the darkness? More medical tests indicated the same person had committed both slayings.

Another theory was that Peter Hi-ma-dan had committed the murders, that his wife had lied to clear him.

Even Simon's father Nah-Gun was accused by the grapevine. As one story put it, "The old man was packed with a war-like spirit and he was quick to fight. He was, like his son and Peter Hi-ma-dan, an expert shot with the rifle. He would have no compunction whatever in killing McIntosh and LeClair, or anyone else for that matter, if his freedom and life were threatened. Furthermore it was attested by witnesses that he had told Gun-an-Noot that LeClair and McIntosh were dead. He had said this long before the bodies had been found. How could he have known if he had been at his ranch as he had testified? It was evident that the quick accusation of Gun-an-Noot had upset his plan. He had expected the killing to remain a mystery. Instead, his son was being blamed. Was that why he planned Gun-an-Noot's flight?"

Perhaps the most intriguing possibility is that unconsciously(?) offered by Corporal Cline in his account. When awaiting Simon's surrender at Hazelton, he had noticed lawyer Henderson to be very agitated and wondered if Simon "*had done some more shooting.*"

Remembering the bullet wounds of the murdered men—"hit in the back about two inches from the spine, the bullet going upward to exit under the collar bone"—the conclusion of Cline's report reads, "During the years that I knew him (Simon), I never questioned him regarding the murders and he never volunteered any information. I am without any actual clue as to who was the guilty party unless the following fact could be accepted as such.

"Simon was a mighty hunter, a crack shot, and invariably shot his game through the spine just back of the shoulders. He claimed that this always dropped the animal in its tracks and spoiled very little meat."   ●

13

THE FLYING DUTCHMAN

Whether, in fact, he had ever been as he claimed, a member of the notorious "Wild Bunch" of Butch Cassidy fame, remains a question for the history books.

But few familiar with his record in British Columbia—brief though it was—doubt for a minute but that Henry Wagner was himself as wild as any of the Hole in the Wall gang which once terrorized the American West. So wild was he, that he became known throughout the Pacific Northwest as the "Flying Dutchman" for his lightning strikes upon coastal communities.

Ironically, if ever Wagner had ridden with Cassidy, Kid Curry and Company, he had certainly changed his modus operandi upon arriving in British Columbia. For here, instead of pillaging the countryside on horseback, Wagner chose to strike from a speedy powerboat, hitting shores along the Gulf of Georgia without warning, and vanishing into the maze of fog and fjords which forms the province's Inside Passage.

It was this unique method that he used during his final, fatal skirmish with authority. Tragically, the outcome of this last hit-and-run attack resulted in the death of a police officer, and a date with the hangman for the Flying Dutchman...

* * *

There is little today to indicate that Union Bay, south of Courtenay, V.I., ever boasted more than its few existing buildings and homes. But, at the turn of the century, Union Bay blossomed into prominence as the shipping port for Cumberland coal, ships from around the world anchoring here to await their turn at its busy loading docks. Daily, railroad cars heaped high with the rich black fuel were shunted along the massive trestle-wharf to empty their cargoes into the yawning holds and bunkers of visiting ships, the waiting squareriggers forming a forest of masts and spars in the bay.

Crowding the low benchland which parallels the Island Highway, then but a wagon track, was the village of Union Bay, where hundreds of homes stood elbow-to-elbow behind the small business section. Dominating this domestic scene was Fraser & Bishop's handsome two-storey store and post office with its imposing gable. Alongside was the Union Bay branch of the Royal Bank of Canada.

But, three-quarters of a century after, the town of Union Bay has almost vanished, the harbor facilities which once operated steadily having been demolished. No longer do beautiful ships of sail call here. When the mines at Cumberland ceased production, the tracks and trestles were ripped up, the historic coke ovens pulled down, brick by brick. Now only acres of slag recall the day when coal meant around-the-clock activity and prosperity to Union Bay—and drew the Flying Dutchman to his fate on the gallows.

Daily, hundreds of cars drive by the crumbling Fraser & Bishop general store. Years have passed since it was last open for business, and a for sale sign feebly attempts to catch the eye of those passing. At last report, it apparently was being used for a small boat building operation, its boarded-up windows assuring occupants, whatever their business, complete privacy.

But if the old store is an eyesore to many, and its days are numbered, it can at least comfort itself with the knowledge that it has a story to tell: a story of a wild night of 60 years ago, when a desperate outlaw and a burly police officer fought a barefisted duel—almost to the death—within its walls. . . .

It had been raining, that fateful midnight of March 3, 1913, when the two police officers standing in the drizzling shelter of a maple spotted the light. Grasping his partner's arm, the one motioned toward Fraser & Bishop's, locked and in darkness. For several seconds, both men peered intently at the building, hearing only the sound of the rain and the nearby surf as Union Bay slept, undisturbed. Provincial Constable Harry Westaway was about to tell his companion, fellow rookie Gordon Ross, that he had been mistaken, when both observed the unmistakeable flicker of a light within the blackened store.

For night after uncomfortable night, in fair weather and

foul, the two young constables had stood watch in the shadows, waiting for the phantom robber to strike, as he had twice before. But, night after night, their only reward had been the cold, stiff muscles and boredom. Each morning, Union Bay would awaken and go to work as the weary officers trudged to their beds. Sometimes morning would bring word from Chief Constable David Stephenson, responsible for the vast lonely region between Alberni and Quatsino, on the Island's northwestern cape—a region comprising almost 8,000 square miles—that another isolated coastal community had been raided during the night.

But Union Bay, which offered not only a tempting target in the form of Fraser & Bishop's store, but an easy getaway due to the fact that it was less than a hundred yards from the beach, remained undisturbed after the pirate's initial raid.

For that matter, Stephenson had no real reason to believe that Union Bay would be hit again, other than a hunch—a gut feeling that, sooner or later, the seaborne robber would yield to the temptation to try his luck there just once more—when Stephenson's men would be waiting for him.

Thus it was, on that wet and dismal midnight of March 3, that the constables stood watch beneath a maple tree. Thus it was that, after hours of waiting, Westaway noticed the telltale glow of a flashlight reflecting off a window of the store.

For several seconds, they watched the eerie glow without moving, quietly debating whether to approach the store themselves, or inform their immediate superior, Const. "Big Mac" J. McKenzie. McKenzie had other matters to attend to on his beat, and had left the nightly ritual of surveillance to his two temporary assistants, checking upon them from time to time. Westaway and Ross had expected him to appear before now, but McKenzie had not showed. Consequently, after brief consultation, the pair decided to enter the store by way of the post office, for which McKenzie had issued them a key.

Crouching low, and avoiding the puddles, they crept alongside the building. Unarmed, Ross held a nightstick in one hand, a flashlight in the other, Westaway, revolver drawn, taking the lead after cautiously unlocking the post office.

Once inside, they tiptoed to the door leading into the store, Ross boldly stepping through and snapping on his flash, its powerful beam almost exploding in the darkness. For a fraction of a second, the officers could see nothing beyond the crowded shelves and counter, when, suddenly, the sweeping light revealed two men, crouched behind the counter—and reflected off the polished barrel of the nearest burglar's Colt.

Acting almost by reflex, Ross dropped the flashlight and

lunged forward, Westaway at his heels. But neither officer had taken two steps before the intruder fired, his .44 slug tearing through the muscle of Ross' shoulder and planting itself squarely in Westaway's chest, knocking that constable backward, unconscious, to the floor.

Despite the sudden pain of his injured shoulder, Ross completed his charge, tackling the gunman as Westaway collapsed, the second burglar taking advantage of the confusion to escape in the darkness, leaving his companion, who had fired the shot, to handle Ross.

Racked with pain, the tough Scotsman grappled with his assailant, neither man being able to see his opponent in the blackness, and both struggling for an advantage. A veteran of the Boer War, Ross was tall and strapping, noted for his strength and marksmanship, but he instantly realized that, although he could not see him, his opponent was husky and had muscles of steel.

Almost 20 years ago, Cecil Clark, former deputy commissioner of the B.C. Provincial Police, vividly described the life-and-death struggle which ensued: "There and then, in the pitch black of Fraser & Bishop's store, was waged one of the greatest man-to-man battles in western police history. A groping, blind, insensate struggle for mastery... The policeman knew the armed robber meant murder, and the desperado, thinking the policeman armed, knew he would use his gun if he could reach it. In the meantime, to Ross the one danger was that deadly .44, which he was trying, with all the strength of his desperation, to twist out of the intruder's grip."

But, for all of his struggling, Ross could not gain an advantage—rather, he found himself, slowly but surely, losing the battle to his powerful antagonist, the latter having succeeded in grabbing him about the throat. When the policeman, almost frantic, attempted to break the other's hold, by jamming his fist into his mouth, the outlaw did not even slacken his death-grip on Ross' windpipe, and added to the constable's agony by clamping down on his fingers, biting through to the bone.

Almost overcome by pain, Ross was forced to release his hold of the burglar's gun hand. Using it as a club, the robber viciously pistol-whipped the policeman, almost blinding him. Still, Ross would not surrender, and, remembering his nightstick, he returned the other's attack, blow for blow. Both men, now bleeding and reeling, staggered back and forth in the darkened store.

From somewhere in the blackness, Westaway groaned, then was silent, the others being too engrossed in their battle to hear him.

Although the duel could have lasted but minutes, to Ross it had seemed an eternity, his overpowering antagonist steadily gaining the advantage and increasing the pressure upon his windpipe, using the other hand to bring down the deadly pistol barrel, again and again and again.

It was Ross' billystick that dramatically turned the tide, when, changing tactic, the officer rammed the end of the club with the last of his waning strength into the outlaw's midriff. With a sudden agonized grunt, the intruder stopped cold, a breathless Ross feeling the vise-grip upon his throat slacken. When the winded burglar sagged to the floor, Ross collapsed on top of him. For all of his pain, he remembered his handcuffs, and feeling for the other's hand, snapped the cold steel bracelet upon a wrist.

As if at a signal, the man heaved upward, knocking Ross away, and struggled to his knees. But he was too slow, Ross having beaten him to his feet, and, raising his arm full height, he brought his nightstick down upon the man's head with all of his might.

With a sickening thud, the leather-bound club connected with the burglar's skull, the impact jarring Ross' arm right to the elbow. But the battle was ended. This time, the outlaw was down for good, sprawling amid a pile of damaged goods like a broken rag doll.

For long minutes, the constable did not move, sagging limply over his prisoner, unable to stir. Finally he forced himself upright. Blinded by the blood flowing from a dozen scalp wounds, and in the darkness, he could not see a foot in front of him. Shuffling forward, arms outstretched, he felt the cold smoothness of a window pane, and smashed it with his stick.

Seconds later, Const. McKenzie, having heard the shattering of glass, was on the scene, shouldering his way through the front door. Upon bursting into the store, he found Const. Ross, whom he scarcely recognized, and his unconscious prisoner, whose bloodied, swollen features, as did those of Ross, grimly testified as to the intensity of their struggle.

To one side lay the still form of Const. Harry Westaway. Even as he felt for a pulse, McKenzie knew that there was no helping the young officer.

Then Chief Constable Stephenson arrived from Nanaimo. Staring at the killer, who lay, still groggy and stiff, on a cell cot, Stephenson pondered the hideous pulp of torn and bruised flesh that was the prisoner's face. But, for all of his injuries, there was no mistaking his powerful frame, close-cropped hair and burning eyes. Const. Ross had captured none other than the Flying Dutchman!

With grim fascination, Stephenson studied the notorious outlaw, now doomed to the gallows for slaying a policeman. As Wagner stared back, blackened eyes glowering with hostility and pain, the officer recalled the circular on his desk which outlined the so-called Dutchman's career as a cattle rustler and highwayman with the Wild Bunch in Wyoming, and his flight to B.C. after a bloody campaign by law officers and the U.S. Cavalry had finally put an end to the gang's marauding. More recently, Wagner had been involved in a shooting in Washington, when he had turned his talents to ransacking isolated Gulf of Georgia communities with partner Bill Julian in a stolen speedboat.

For his part in the burglaries, Julian, who surrendered without a fight when tracked to his Lasqueti Island cabin, was sentenced to five years. For killing Const. Harry Westaway, Henry Wagner was sentenced to die, Aug. 25, 1913.

On that summer morning, the heavily shackled prisoner, whose final days in a death cell had been marked by repeated attempts at suicide, mounted the gallows in the Nanaimo jailyard. Showing the effects of his confinement, Wagner was bearded, his hair long and shaggy. But, refusing to betray any emotion, he faced the end stoically, as, from among the small gallery of spectators, Const. Ross watched the notorious outlaw who had killed his colleague and friend, and who had almost killed him.

Seconds later, the condemned murderer plunged earthward. The Flying Dutchman, cattle rustler, gunslinger, pirate and killer, was a part of history—another fascinating outlaw of the Canadian frontier...

In May of 1971, at a Victoria exhibition marking Canadian Police Week, a highlight of the display was the single-action Colt .44 used by Wagner to shoot Const. Westaway. A second macabre memento of the past was a piece of heavy hemp—the rope used to hang the Flying Dutchman at Nanaimo, 58 years before.   ●

14

THE WILD MCLEANS

A black day when death rode the rangeland was commemorated by British Columbians in August of 1967, when a silent crowd witnessed the unveiling of a cairn, near Kamloops. Erected in memory of John Tannatt Ussher, the memorial recalled the heroic constable gunned down by the marauding McLean Brothers, most notorious outlaws in provincial history.

It was back in December, 1879, that Ussher fell in the line of duty, but the reign of terror actually had begun much earlier—almost as far back as when the McLeans had learned to shoot. According to an old account: "They were all of a wild, reckless disposition, and being good horsemen and capital shots, preferred enjoying a roving life to any settled employment."

The desperate band consisted of 25-year-old Allen McLean, leader, his brothers Charlie, 17, Archie 15, and another halfbreed, Alex Hare, 17. Deadly experts with rifle, revolver and hunting knife, they were "the true product of a wild frontier existence."

Ironically, the McLeans seemed predestined to meet violent ends.

Their father, Donald McLean, was little short of a monster. The most outstanding event in the Hudson's Bay Company trader's dark career occurred in 1849, when he led a 16-man posse after a Chilcotin Indian brave named Tlel, suspected of murdering company servant Alexis Belanger.

After his men surrounded Tlel's cabin, where the city of Quesnel now stands, McLean, armed with two pistols and a musket, burst through the door. The snarling trader found the fugitive's uncle, stepdaughter and her baby. When the frightened old man swore he did not know where Tlel was hiding, McLean, beside himself with insane fury, shouted, "Then for today you shall be Tlel!"

Drawing both pistols, he fired point-blank, but, in his frenzy, missed. Grabbing his musket, he jammed the barrel into the unarmed native's midriff and jerked the trigger. The heavy ball slammed the old man against the wall, killing him instantly.

Alarmed at the shots, Tlel charged from another room to be "repeatedly shot until he fell lifeless." Also alarmed by the shooting was a member of the posse waiting outside, who leaped through the doorway and fired at the squaw. His shot passed through the baby, killing it, and buried itself in the mother's shoulder. This last atrocity, it is encouraging to note, is considered an accident.

Tlel's tribe swore to avenge the massacre, but it took 14 years and several ambushes before Donald McLean met his just—and overdue—desserts at the hands of a Chilcotin brave. Examination of the trader's riddled body revealed why previous attempts had failed—McLean wore a bulletproof vest. The assassin had succeeded when he switched tactics, firing from behind.

As if the blood of fiery McLean were not enough to hint of future violence, the young brothers inherited the brooding temperament of their mother's people, the Kamloops tribe.

The boys began sowing their wild oats early, committing "some depredations in the way of horse and cattle stealing..." Strangely, says an early report, authorities seemed reluctant to take them seriously. A lethal mistake, for "impunity led to excesses, and at last complaints were lodged against them with the magistrates in the vicinity. Some of them were captured, but so great was the reluctance to punish them that they were allowed to escape."

But finally came the day when their activities could no longer be regarded as youthful exuberance; and with this fateful realization began the wildest manhunt the province has ever known.

Final straw had been the gang's theft of a prized black stallion belonging to Kamloops rancher, Bill Palmer. The angry cowman had immediately saddled up and tracked his animal. However, when he rode up on the evil quartet he realized discretion to be the better part of valor and pretended to ignore his former property.

The cocky rustlers had greeted him with open amusement, enjoying his about-face to the hilt. But Palmer was not thinking of his wounded pride when they allowed him to retreat; as he later told Const. Ussher, he was convinced they had been hoping he would show his hand, thereby giving them an excuse to shoot him. All had been drinking and were heavily armed with Colts and rifles.

Ussher listened quietly to the rancher's complaint, as he had to so many before, then reached for his stetson. Swearing in Palmer as a special constable, and a veteran tracker named Shumway, he galloped in pursuit. Under Shumway's expert guidance, the little posse, now reinforced by another rancher, John McLeod, had little difficulty following the gang's trail.

It was snowing and getting dark, late December 8, when they finally spotted the outlaw's fire. Squinting against the falling snow, Ussher could see bedrolls laid out beside the fire, the horses, including Palmer's stallion, hobbled beyond. But there was not a sign of the McLeans or Hare.

The constable raised his hand to wave his men forward. Without warning, the rustlers opened fire, blasting from behind trees and brush. A pistol ball shattered McLeod's cheek, although, amazingly, it missed his teeth. The heroic rancher, retching on his own blood, fought to stay in the saddle as his wounded horse bucked in terror. As if he were not busy enough he managed to fire both barrels of his shotgun, when hit in the leg.

In seconds, it had become carnage; as buckshot, rifle and pistol ball whistled through the dusk. By now only McLeod was firing back. Shumway was unarmed, Ussher's pistol remained in its saddle holster; he and Palmer had their hands full just trying to control their crazed mounts. The rancher did not realize until after that a shot had amputated most of his frozen beard.

The real tragedy was Const. Ussher's complete misjudgement of the wanted youths. Probably remembering the many times he had hauled them in, suffering nothing more than their curses, he decided to try talking them into surrendering before anyone was seriously hurt. It was a fatal error.

Leaping from his horse, unarmed, Ussher ran toward Alex Hare. The wiry halfbreed had exposed himself to take better aim at the officer but, before he could shoot, Ussher had him in a bear-like grip. The constable was stronger, but Hare was quicker. As Ussher grappled for the gun, Hare's free hand clutched desperately for his knife. Slipping the hunting blade under Ussher's mackinaw, he heaved with all his strength. The stricken lawman groaned and fell back. As Hare drove his

blade into the writhing body a few more times, Archie McLean
raced to his side and fired, blasting away most of Ussher's
face.

Upon seeing his fate, the survivors retreated at full gallop to
Kamloops. As McLeod received medical attention, Shumway
and Palmer breathlessly gave the gory details to Justice of the
Peace John Clapperton, sole legal authority after the constable's death.

News of the cold-blooded murder instantly changed the quiet
cowtown into a hive of seething hatred. For miles around,
ranchers grabbed rifles and shotguns, armed their hired
hands, and headed for town to join the posse. Righteous anger
became desperate determination when it was rumored the
outlaws were gathering arms for the savage Nicola Indians to
lead them in rebellion. Many had vivid memories of the brief
but bloody uprising of the fierce Chilcotins, 17 years before.

Clapperton wired provincial police headquarters at Victoria
for instructions. After an emergency conference with Attorney-General G.A. Walkem, Police Superintendent Charles
Todd telegraphed Const. James Lindsay, at Barkerville.
Lindsay was to meet Const. Tunstall at Cache Creek and speed
to Kamloops. Washington Territory authorities were alerted to
keep close watch on the border in case the McLeans tried
fleeing the country.

When Justice Clapperton's grim posse rode out on its historic
manhunt, it was to follow an easy trail. Drunk on rotgut
whisky and their first taste of blood, the outlaws left a wake of
death and terror.

Soon the posse reigned in at their abandoned camp. In the
reddened snow lay the pathetic remains of Const. Ussher. The
killers had mutilated his body and stripped it of boots, jacket,
gloves and handcuffs. As they wrapped the stiffened corpse in
a saddle blanket, most of the hunters were thinking of his
young bride; they had been married but a year. Many stroked
cold rifle butts in silence. The McLeans would pay dearly, they
swore to themselves. . . .

At the ranch of Tom Trapp, the posse listened to a
blood-chilling tale of horror. Trapp was still suffering from
shock as he told Clapperton of his visit by the four horsemen of
death.

"They rode right up, grinnin', and without so much as a
howdy told me they just killed Ussher, the constable!" panted
the shaking rancher. "When I said they were drunk, jest
suckin' wind, they showed me his handcuffs—all covered in
blood.

"I tell you, I was scared. That young Archie McLean; I tell

you he's the devil hisself. He wanted to kill me right then and there. But Allen, the oldest, just laughed and pulled a half dollar from his pocket.

"Tails you win—heads you die!" he said, and flipped it into the snow! I tell you, I almost died of fright 'fore I saw it was tails. Lucky for me Allen kept his word. Then...they just rode off..."

An old hog rancher named Roberts was equally lucky. At gunpoint the killers had asked for several old enemies, planning to settle outstanding complaints. "I ain't no idee where they be, boys—I swear!" he quaked. The gang rode on.

Following the trail, the posse neared Trapp Lake. Here they found further evidence the youthful band had become a pack of mad dogs. The gaunt body of an old shepherd named Kelly was sprawled at the foot of a small bluff. Nearby, his sheep foraged in the snow. It did not take an expert tracker to see what had happened: The gang had spotted Kelly from down the trail. The old man probably had not even heard his slayers, let alone seen one raise his rifle. As the carbine shattered the stillness, Kelly spun, dead, from his rocky perch. His battered watch and chain later were found on Alex Hare.

At another ranch, Clapperton heard a now familar account of terror. Once again Allen had good-naturedly spared his frightened hosts, bowing gallantly to the cattleman's wife and daughters. Before riding on, they looted the house of all guns and ammunition.

But time had run out. Their leisurely game of life-or-death was almost over. When the gang finally settled for the night in an abandoned cabin at Douglas Lake, Clapperton's men were right behind. Even as they ripped up floor-boards to strengthen the log walls, the posse was quietly surrounding their shack.

Clapperton waited until his men were in position, then ordered the youths to surrender. He had no intention of making the same mistake as Ussher, delivering his ultimatum from behind a tree. When the fugitives replied with a burst of rifle fire, he had already planned his strategy.

Earlier he had noticed an old horse sleigh in the cabin clearing. He ordered several men to soak it in kerosene and shove it to the cabin, hoping to smoke the wanted men out. Seconds later, the sled was ablaze. Eagerly, the lawmen wrestled with the bulky, flaming rig.

The outlaws immediately realized their intentions, pouring round after round into the sleigh. Suddenly the posse found itself in serious trouble. Few could get a good grip on the vehicle because of the fire, and the flames were exposing them to the killer's broadside. When Clapperton grimly sounded retreat, a raucous cheer erupted from the cabin. Only one lawman had been slightly wounded.

But the gang must have known that, although they had won the first battle, they had not a chance of winning the war. They were surrounded by a well-armed, provisioned posse; morning would bring reinforcements. When the last of their food and water was gone, it was but a matter of time. Clapperton's men could wait indefinitely.

The hours dragged by. A day passed. It was a cold vigil for the posse, huddled about a fire, but they knew it could not last much longer. The second day came and went. It had been a hard chase, cold, wet and miserable, after a pack of mad killers, yet even Clapperton felt little satisfaction when he saw sticks poked through cracks in the cabin wall. They were getting desperate, he knew, if they had to try scooping in snow to drink.

Finally...the end. On the third day, Allen shouted they were coming out. As the posse watched warily, the bullet-scarred door moved slightly, then swung wide. A white rag appeared, then its owner stepped nervously into the clearing. One, two, three followed. The four youths stood undecided, blinking shyly at their hunters.

Suddenly, with a fierce whoop, Allen raised his rifle skyward and fired. As the posse watched in awe, the halfbreeds emptied their carbines into the grey heavens. Indian code demanded a brave fight until his last cartridge. The manhunt had ended.

After the preliminary hearing at Kamloops, the sullen outlaws were shackled to their horses for the cold journey to New Westminster. In single file, the prisoners and three-man escort struggled through treacherous Fraser Canyon during a blizzard. At Yale the convoy switched to canoes to continue downriver. Heavy ice, however, meant another change of plan, this time to a straw-cushioned wagon. The quartet finally completed the four-day trip to prison on foot, having to hike across the frozen Fraser to the provincial jail. It was Christmas Day, 1879.

One of the officers escorting the manacled prisoners on the grim journey was a constable named Burr; a descendant is Raymond Burr, television's popular Perry Mason and "Ironside."

Found guilty of first degree murder, they were sentenced to death. A successful appeal caused a second trial. Again, the verdict was guilty. This time there was no reprieve. On the icy morning of January 31, 1881, Allen, Charlie and Archie McLean, with sidekick Alexander Hare, shuffled into the grey prison yard for the last time. Minutes later, it was over.

Ironically, even in death the murderous McLeans made Canadian criminal history. Archie is among the youngest ever executed, and it is believed the only time three brothers have been hanged together.

Four years later, the dreaded name of McLean again made headlines. Stepbrother Alexander recalled his notorious kin when he ran wild on the Kamloops reserve. The beserk gunman claimed one dead and four wounded before his grandfather, Chief Louie, and a posse in full war paint blasted him into eternity.

Still another McLean was to make international news. For eldest brother, Allen, had left an infant son. George McLean's Highland and Indian blood surged to the fore in France, during World War I, when the heroic sergeant singlehandedly charged a vital German position at bloody Vimy Ridge with a handful of grenades. When the smoke cleared, young George had killed 19 and captured 21 officers and men, winning himself the DCM. •

15

ANTOINE LUCANAGE

"The so-called whisky was the vilest stuff that the ingenuity of wicked-minded and avaricious white men ever concocted. What it was composed of was known only to the concoctors. I was told that it was made of alcohol diluted with water toned up with an extract of red pepper and colored so as to resemble the real thing. It was conveyed to the reserve under cover of night by boatloads.

"What the Indians wanted was something hot—something that would burn holes through his unaccustomed stomach and never stop burning holes until it reached his heels. Quality was not considered. The rotgut must be cheap as well as pungent, and these two elements being present, the sale was rapid and profitable..."

This, in the words of a pioneer journalist, was the poison that was sold by the boatload to the Indians of British Columbia. Although selling liquor to Indians was illegal, it was a lucrative trade, conducted, for the most part, under cover of darkness, by unscrupulous traders; many of whom were respected citizens by day. For years, Victoria was the headquarters of the illicit whisky trade with the natives, sloops, rowboats and dugouts ferrying thousands of gallons of rotgut to thirsty customers.

Where once an advanced culture had ruled the length of the West Coast, "debauchery, outrage and death" marched unchecked, as "tanglefoot," or "tangleleg," whisky stalked man, women and child from Washington Territory to Alaska. Then, what whisky had begun, disease ended. More than epidemic, more than the white man's advanced ways, liquor destroyed the complex Indian culture, his integrity and independence.

Despite the efforts of the authorities, the illegal whisky trade flourished for years. From wholesale liquor import warehouses at the foot of Victoria's Johnson Street, thousands of gallons of the vile liquid were smuggled upcoast, where eager customers waited anxiously to pay hard cash for slow death. The addicted brave usually paid a dollar a bottle; each sale of the diluted death meaning a 90 percent profit for the peddlar.

Among the disreputables who willingly risked imprisonment to meet this demand for drink was 35-year-old Antoine Lucanage, a pock-marked, shifty-eyed and shambling French Canadian who worked out of Bella Coola. Profits were high, and the risks reasonably slight and, for a time, like many others, "Antoine," as he was better known, made a profitable career of supplying the Indians with tanglefoot.

The authorities did their best to control the whisky trade but, considering the hundreds of miles of lonely coastline, and the scarcity of policemen, it was an impossible task. One of the handful of officers who did his best to stop the traffic was John D. B. Ogilvie, Deputy Collector of Customs and Indian Agent at Bella Coola.

On May 23, 1865, the Hudson's Bay Company steamer *Labouchere* docked at Victoria with a large passenger list and cargo. Capt. Lewis also brought intelligence of "the melancholy death of Mr. Ogilvie."

Seven weeks earlier, said Lewis, the renegade known as Antoine had landed at Bella Coola with three kegs of liquor in his canoe. As Lucanage lacked a permit, Bella Coola customs officer Jack Ogilvie seized both Antoine and liquor; placing the former aboard the steamer, *Nanaimo Packet*, to be taken to New Westminster for trial.

But Lucanage escaped from the *Packet* and flagged down the northbound schooner, *Langley*, whose master obligingly dropped him off—at Bella Coola—where the fugitive announced it as being his intention to head for Cariboo. Ogilvie thought otherwise: that the bootlegger was merely hiding in the woods until the schooner's southbound trip, when he planned to sneak back aboard.

Days later, the *Langley* headed down Bentinck Arm against a stiff headwind. Four hours after, Ogilvie, Morris Moss, a man named Smith, and four Indians, paddled in pursuit; overtaking the laboring vessel late that night. Hailing her master, that officer assured them that Lucanage was not aboard, that he had not seen the fugitive since he left the schooner at Bella Coola on the northbound run.

Upon accepting his word, the posse also accepted his invitation to go below for dinner. Once they were aboard, he offered to go forward to light a fire for tea, Ogilvie volunteering to assist. The captain was just firing the stove, Ogilvie sitting alongside, when Lucanage, who had hidden himself in a fo'c'sle locker, fired without a word of warning at the unsuspecting customs officer.

Hearing the shot, Moss and Smith, who had remained in the main cabin, rushed topside, where they met the mortally wounded Ogilvie. He told them that Lucanage had shot him, then collapsed on deck, where he asked for a drink of water.

By this time, the captain, according to the report, charged on deck "in a fearful state of excitement, and did not appear to know what he was doing. Mr. Moss asked him for a lantern to go down and seize Antoine, but he said there was none on board. He was then told to put the schooner about and run her back to Bella Coola, but not doing so at once, Mr. Moss went aft for that purpose, leaving Mr. Smith to attend to Mr. Ogilvie."

No sooner had Moss headed aft than Lucanage rushed on deck and, taking Smith by surprise, stabbed him twice, then turned upon the dying Ogilvie. That officer, with his remaining strength, managed to wrest the gun from Lucanage's hand, at which his attacker hastened down the companionway, Ogilvie speeding his retreat with two shots from his assassin's gun.

Astern, Moss had heard the latest commotion and, seeing Lucanage, raised his own gun to fire—when the arching boom knocked him over the side. Fortunately, he was rescued by the Indians who had abandoned ship in their canoe at the first shot.

Back aboard the schooner, the captain and his mate assisted the wounded men below, and ignored Lucanage, who seized the opportunity to escape in the ship's boat. Upon returning topside, the master fired four times, but missed, then shouted to Moss, who was in the Indian canoe and too far off to hear him.

The next day, Moss returned with reinforcements, Ogilvie breathing his last an hour later. His body was then returned to Bella Coola by canoe, to await shipment to Victoria, where Ogilvie had asked to be interred.

Lucanage, meanwhile, had vanished. But Moss had more pressing problems of his own, having to escort two Indian prisoners to New Westminster. Two weeks after, he was appointed customs officer in Ogilvie's place.

Immediately upon receiving word of Ogilvie's death, the provincial government offered a reward for his capture:

$1000 REWARD

WHEREAS, ON THE 6TH DAY OF MAY, instant, John D.B. Ogilvy [sic], Esquire, Deputy Collector of Customs and Indian Agent, was wilfully murdered on board the schooner "Langley," at Bentinck Arm.

One thousand dollars is hereby offered for the apprehension of Antoine Lucanage, commonly known on the Coast as "Antoine," who is accused of the muder of the said J.D.B. Ogilvy.

The reward will be paid to any persons handing over the said "Antoine" to any Police authority of British Columbia.

By His Excellency's Command, C. BREW, Chief Inspector of Police, New Westminster, 20th May, 1865.

DESCRIPTION OF "ANTOINE"

Height about 5 ft. 10 ins., very thin, pitted with the smallpox, light hair and eyes, about 35 years of age, stoops slightly when walking speaks English well [with] slight foreign accent, slight moustache and whiskers.

When next Lucanage was heard of, he was reported to have been seen at Fort Rupert, near the northern tip of Vancouver Island, by the master of the trading schooner, *Nonpareil*. Upon his arrival in Victoria, the captain declared that he had seen the killer eight days earlier, but, at the time, had not been aware of Ogilvie's slaying. According to his information, Antoine had reached Fort Rupert by canoe, having promised his Indian boatmen eight blankets if they would "take him down quick."

However, once at the trading post, Antoine had heard that the vessel *Jemmy Jones* was anchored on the opposite side of the island, and "he skedadled for that point at once, leaving his Indians in the lurch...!" Upon learning of the murder of Ogilvie, the *Nonpareil*'s master had informed the captain of the gunboat, HMS *Chameleon*.

A further 10 days passed without further word of the murderer's whereabouts, when a man named Sebastopol— "the well-known and indefatigable prospector"—arrived from the northwest coast. To a newspaper reporter, Sebastopol stated that "he thinks he discovered some faint traces of the murderer of Mr. Ogilvy (sic). While lying in shore in Queen Charlotte Sound, during a storm, he saw a canoe with two or three men pass down paddling vigorously against a head wind. He and his party of Indians hailed the canoe, and fired guns to attract their attention, but they continued their course. As Indians rarely travel in such a hurry in stormy weather,

Sebastopol surmised that some white man must have been in the canoe.

"On arriving at Fort Rupert he learned that Antoine had been there, which rendered it probable that he was in the canoe seen in Queen Charlotte Sound. On Friday last, while on his way down from Fort Rupert, shortly after passing Salmon River, Sebastopol and his party were hailed by a white man from the shore. He wished to land and see who it was, but some of the Indians were afraid, and he was therefore reluctantly obliged to proceed, although the voice called three or four times. Sebastopol thinks it not unlikely that the man was Antoine. It was stated yesterday that someone paid a large sum to two men on Wednesday night to be landed on the other (American) side and it was thought that it might possibly have been Antoine, but it is unlikely that rascal could have any money at his disposal."

Then the manhunt was ended, it being reported that Governor Frederick Seymour had received a telegram, from officials in San Francisco, to the effect that the killer was in the Bay City and under police surveillance. As the Victoria *Colonist* optimistically reported Antoine's capture, provincial chief of police Chartres Brew boarded the steamer *Leviathan* for Victoria. In his satchel he carried the necessary papers for Antoine's extradition, but arrived too late to make the connection with the mail steamer and, so as not to lose any more time, decided to go overland.

A day later, a traveller from Port Townsend arrived in Victoria, to state that Antoine had been seen in that Puget Sound port on the first and second days of July. According to this informant, the killer had reached that city by canoe and stayed in an unoccupied shanty. There was no question of his identity, said the traveller, as the pilot of the steamer *Eliza Anderson*, "who knew him well," had talked to him. No attempt had been made to arrest him on the American side as officials there had not been formally instructed to take action. Antoine then had proceeded to Port Discovery, where he hoped to ship on board the bark *Lucy Ann*; only to find that she had already sailed for San Francisco. "...He accordingly seems," reported the *Colonist*, "to have pushed on to Port Angeles, where he probably met the bark or some other vessel, on the point of sailing for the Bay City and managed to secure a passage."

Chief Brew made it only as far as Monticello, when he was instructed by wire to return to New Westminster, as B.C. authorities had been informed by San Francisco police that Antoine had slipped from sight.

For two and a half months, all efforts to trace the fugitive were unsuccessful. Antoine Lucanage had dropped out of view, and it was with some surprise that he was run to earth in October. Ironically, it was then learned that his flight had ended almost as soon as it had begun. For Antoine was dead; his skeletal remains having been found near Fort Rupert, and positively identified by his revolver. Only then was it learned that the Indian canoemen whom Antoine had hired to take him to Rupert had killed him when he failed to make good his promise of eight blankets.

Today, more than a century afterward, Antoine Lucanage, bootlegger and murderer, is long forgotten. But the name of his victim, Jack Ogilvie, lives on, Victoria's Burnside Street recalling his farm on the Gorge waterway. Provincially, Ogilvie is remembered for having started British Columbia's million-dollar honey industry by importing the province's first honey bees, in 1858. •

16

ERNEST CASHEL

Crime, it would seem, has a way of snowballing. For 22-year-old Ernest Cashel of Wyoming, graduation from petty thief and forger to outlaw and murderer came in the fall of 1902.

Cashel, who was on the run for theft and jailbreak in his home state, first attracted the attention of the Calgary city police on October 14, when he passed a worthless cheque. When the youthful badman made a break for the prairie, by jumping through a washroom window of the train taking him back to Calgary, the Mounted Police took up the chase. A week passed without sign of the fugitive, until he stole a pony outside Lacombe and the manhunt was concentrated in that region. But, again, Cashel went underground and a month passed.

Police were reminded of the missing forger and horse thief when a Pleasant Valley settler, D. A. Thomas, reported his brother-in-law to be missing. J. R. Belt, said Thomas, had a ranch about 40 miles east of Lacombe, and was last seen about the first of November. Since then, he had not heard from his brother-in-law, the ranch was deserted, and none of the 47-year-old Belt's neighbors could offer a clue as to his whereabouts.

From neighboring farmers, Const. McLeod confirmed that the rancher had last been seen about the first week of November, when he had taken in a young man who had given his name as Bert Elseworth. A check of Belt's sod-roofed cabin revealed that most of the rancher's personal effects, including his horse, saddle, shotgun, clothing and a 50-dollar gold certificate, were missing. As neither man had been seen since, McLeod became convinced that the rancher had met with foul play, and concentrated his investigation upon the young transient.

When Belt's neighbors described Elseworth as being in his early 20s, of slender build, with long dark hair and sideburns, McLeod realized with a start that "Bert Elseworth" must be Ernest Cashel, wanted by Calgary police for forgery and breaking jail.

This, McLeod reported to Supt. Sanders. As yet, they had no body and could not state for certain that Belt had actually been murdered. Nevertheless, convinced that Cashel had murdered his host so as to rob him, Sanders decided to call in the force's best-known detective.

Thirty-four-years-old, born in India, and formally an officer in the British army, Const. Alex Pennycuick, the "Sherlock Holmes of the NWMP," had made his mark as a detective while posted to the Yukon during the Klondike rush, when he had—literally—moved mountains to solve a triple slaying.

This famous case began when three travellers on the Dawson trail vanished in December of 1899. When Cpl. Paddy Ryan of the Hootchiku detachment discovered that the travellers' disappearance was linked with a series of food thefts in the Fort Yukon area, he turned the case over to Const. Pennycuick of that detachment. Upon examining an abandoned campsite found by Ryan, Pennycuick identified the stove as belonging to two English drifters whom he had suspected for some time of having broken into miners' caches.

He immediately wired their description to the border crossing of Tagish. Two days later, a man giving his name as George O'Brien reported in at the NWMP checkpoint, enroute to Alaska. As he answered the description of one of the suspected thieves, and had served time in Dawson City, he was detained, and police began to look for his partner, and fellow convict, Tommy Graves.

Sure now that O'Brien and Graves were behind the disappearance of the travellers, Pennycuick, and a private detective who had been hired by a brother of one of the missing men, began to retrace O'Brien's movements along the Dawson trail. It was the middle of winter, but the two men systematically examined every foot of the trail for 16 bitter, exhausting miles. At the junction of the Yukon River and Pork Trails, near the site of the abandoned camp, they found what appeared to have been an ambush site. Shortly after, one of their dogs was attracted by a slight depression and, carefully scraping away the snow, the detectives found bloodstains.

For six incredible, wearying and frigid weeks, the pair ignored the numbing cold to examine every square foot of a four-acre site; sifting their way through more than three feet of snow to uncover a blood-curdling array of evidence: human remains, patches of frozen blood, a bullet-chipped tooth, spent cartridges and, in ashes of the fire, charred remains of clothing and a pair of moccasins.

It was, in the words of one historian, one of the most thorough investigations in the history of crime detection. But it remained for the spring thaw of 1900 before Pennycuick and partner McGuire were able to confirm their theory of ambush and murder. With the breakup of the Yukon River ice, they recovered the bullet-ridden bodies of the missing travellers—as well as that of O'Brien's partner and cellmate, Tommy Graves.

Other evidence proved conclusively that O'Brien and Graves had made camp at the junction of the trails and waited for the first likely looking victims. Then they had gunned down the three travellers, and thrown their bodies through a hole chopped in the ice; when O'Brien had dissolved the partnership by disposing of Graves. At his trial, he could not dispute the overwhelming mass of circumstantial evidence that Pennycuick and McGuire had gathered at the ambush site; the two even having matched the shard of tooth to one of the victims. Within two hours, O'Brien was found guilty and sentenced to hang. He went to his death, it was reported, cursing the NWMP constable whose patience and determination had solved what well could have been a "perfect crime."

Two years later, the case of the missing rancher, Rufus Belt, offered Const. Pennycuick a similar challenge. As in the O'Brien case, the *corpus delecti* had not been found immediately, and, with the same determination and perseverance he had shown in the Yukon, he proceeded to approach the case from the angle of the missing body.

In the meantime, the search for Ernest Cashel went on. In mid-January of 1903, some two and a half months since Belt vanished, a man answering Cashel's description borrowed a horse from a Jumping Pound rancher named Healy. At Kananaskis, the fugitive abandoned the horse, stole a diamond ring, then hopped a freight train as far as Canmore. By this time, the police were again on his trail, and were informed by the train crew that the caboose had been entered and some clothing stolen. From Canmore, Cashel made his way to Anthracite—and right into the arms of Const. Blyth. When arrested, he was carrying the diamond ring, and wearing a pair of corduroy trousers which strongly resembled a pair owned by rancher Belt.

However, for all of Const. Pennycuick's efforts to date, Cashel could not be conclusively linked to Belt's disappearance, and it was on the minor charges of having stolen the ring at Kananaskis, and the horse at Lacombe, that Cashel stood trial that spring. On May 14, he was found guilty on both counts and sentenced to three years in Stony Mountain Penitentiary.

But Pennycuick had not given up. With Cashel safely tucked away for three years, he had ample time in which to examine the Belt evidence with his microscopic eye. Painstakingly, he traced the movements of the missing rancher's equally missing boarder, Bert Elseworth, to a half-breed settlement near Calgary. There, he learned that Elseworth had stayed with the inhabitants early in November, and had flashed a 50-dollar gold certificate, such as was known to have been in the possession of J.R. Belt. Even more intriguing was a coat which Elseworth had left with his hosts. Of corduroy, it matched the trousers Cashel had been wearing when arrested, and was identified as having belonged to J.R. Belt.

There no longer was the slightest doubt in Pennycuick's mind but that Cashel and Elseworth were one and the same, and that the young forger and horsethief had murdered and robbed Belt. But, to date, he had not even proved that Belt had been murdered. There was no evidence of violence in the house, and no sign of a hastily-dug grave on the ranch. The obvious place to dispose of a body was the nearby Red River, and, with spring breakup, Pennycuick and Const. Rogers proceeded to drag its length and to search its banks and bars for a stretch of several miles downstream. This task took them several weeks and proved to be fruitless.

And there matters might have remained, had not a farmer 20 miles downriver from the Belt ranch noticed a suspicious looking object drifting with the current. Upon looking closer, he saw that it was a body, dragged it ashore with his rope, wrapped it in a blanket, and sent for the NWMP. Despite the fact that the corpse had been in the river for several months and was badly decomposed, identification was relatively simple. Belt had had a deformed toe on his left foot and had worn an iron-reinforced boot. The left toe of the corpse was deformed, and the boot was reinforced with iron.

Formally identified as that of J. R. Belt, the body carried a third distinguishing mark—a bullet hole near the heart. When Pennycuick extracted the .44 bullet, he found it to be of the same calibre as that of the rifle and revolver taken from Cashel when he was arrested.

With this evidence against him, Cashel went on trial for murder, was readily convicted, and sentenced to die that December.

This should have been the end of the J. R. Belt murder case,
and of Ernest Cashel, but, on December 10, five days before he
was to hang, Ernest received a welcome visitor in his death cell.
The caller, who had travelled all the way from Wyoming, was
his elder brother, John, who brought sympathies from the
Cashel family—and two loaded revolvers. Then, visiting time
having run out, John left the jail, and proceeded to a nearby
street corner, where he had arranged to wait for his brother
with a pair of boots.

Back in the jail, Ernest whipped out the pistols, surprised his
three guards, and, as the alarm was sounded, fled into the night.
He was unable to keep his rendezvous with John, however, as
his brother had been arrested within minutes of his escape.

Once again, Cashel made for the open prairie. This time, Supt.
Sanders was leaving nothing to chance. Already sentenced to
death, Cashel had nothing to lose and was heavily armed, and
Sanders dispatched posses to alert the farmers and ranchers
around Calgary of his escape. Yet, for all of their efforts, the
police could not find the killer and, on December 12, Supt.
Sanders was replaced by Comm. A. Bowen Perry who, with
Insp. Knight, arrived from Regina to take personal command of
the manhunt. Perry also posted a reward of $1,000 for
information leading to Cashel's capture, and ordered every
available man into the field. Eleven days later, the commissioner
had to return to Regina. And Ernest Cashel, forger, horsethief
and murderer, remained at large.

The young outlaw had not been able to remain undetected,
however, as he had been forced to rob several ranches and
Supt. Sanders, who had resumed control of the search,
deduced, by the locations of the victimized ranches, that Cashel
was holed up in the Sheppard district. As the robberies had
occurred at night, it was obvious that Cashel slept during the
day and ventured out only after dusk. Sanders resolved to
search the entire Sheppard district, inch-by-inch, house by
house, cellar by cellar, barn by barn, with an army of police and
specially sworn-in volunteers.

With 20 policemen and 20 armed civilians, Sanders divided
them into five eight-man parties, placed each under the
command of one of his officers and, at 8:30 on the morning of
Jan. 24, 1903, began to scour the region. No outbuilding, no
matter how small or derelick, was overlooked, and even
haystacks were probed with rifle barrel and pitch fork. Three
hours passed uneventfully, until the party led by Insp. A. W.
Duffus arrived at the Pitman ranch.

While the rest of the men searched the grounds, Const. Biggs
proceeded to search the bunkhouse. The ground floor was

empty, but a trapdoor led to a cellar, and Biggs started down the cellar steps. As he descended into the darkness, cautiously feeling for each step, there was a flash, a roar and a loud thud, and a bullet buried itself in the wall beside him. Jerking backward, Biggs fired twice into the blackness, and was answered by more shots, when he beat a hasty retreat to the surface.

Moments later, Duffus was on the scene. Sure now that they had their man trapped in the cellar, the inspector decided against risking any of his men. Instead, he ordered them to burn down the shack. If Cashel emerged firing, they were to shoot to kill. Duffus' instructions were no sooner issued than done. As flames swept through the shanty, the policemen waited with guns at the ready. Soon the shack was ablaze to the rooftop, when a gasping, choking Ernest Cashel burst into the open. His only thought was the fresh air, and the Mounties seized him without a struggle.

On Feb. 2, 1903, nine days after his recapture, and 50 days beyond his original execution date, Ernest Cashel went to the gallows for the murder of J. R. Belt. With his recapture, the Mounties got their man and Const. Alex Pennycuick chalked up another remarkable investigation. •

17

GADDY & RACETTE

Although only 26, Moise Racette looked much older. With his pulled-down Stetson, stooped shoulders, deep-set black eyes, and tight-lipped scowl, he could have passed for 40. By contrast, his friend and partner, James Gaddy, looked deceptively innocent; his round-moon face and cow-lick making him look even younger than his 22 years.

Both men, in terms of experience, were much older than most men their actual years.

Short, stocky and muscular, Racette hailed from Wolseley, Sask. Gaddy, small and slight, came from the Crooked Lakes reserve where, after serving two years of a five-year sentence for horse theft, he returned in 1884 and settled down in marriage. When he met Racette, both men became fast friends; having in common the fact that both had served time at Stony Mountain.

Working at odd jobs, they moved about the countryside; never staying long or doing more than necessary to keep themselves in grub and whisky. The spring of 1887 found them in the Qu'Apelle area, bored and broke. When the boyish-looking Gaddy suggested that they make some easy money by stealing horses, Racette readily agreed. For the venture they needed guns and horses, and the first requirement, two revolvers, were acquired by honest labor. The second necessity, horses, were easier to obtain; the outlaws simply making their way to Moose Jaw, where they stole two ponies and a mare, before heading back to Qu'Appelle.

En route, they came to the homestead of Hector McLeish, a Scottish immigrant. A giant of a man, 30-year-old McLeish was known to his neighbors as one of the strongest men in the district, and one who would not take kindly to having his horse stolen. But this did not bother the outlaws, who calmly made off with one of his animals and headed for Racette's home.

With morning, McLeish found that his animal was gone and, beside himself with rage, he resolved to track the rustlers. When a neighbor named Brown agreed to help him, they followed the outlaws' trail as far as Qu'Appelle, where McLeish reported the theft to Sgt. Tyffe of the NWMP. Tyffe quickly organized a small posse.

By this time it was apparent that the thieves were headed for Wolseley and, as they proceeded, the lawmen questioned settlers along the route, who were able to give detailed descriptions of the wanted men. Finally one of the persons they questioned was able to offer more than a description: the name of Moise Racette.

That night, the posse reached Wolseley, when most of the men retired to a hotel, as Sgt. Tyffe and McLeish consulted with Const. Mathewson of the local detachment. McLeish, however, was impatient to recover his horse. When Mathewson informed him that the Racette place was only a mile out of town, the angry Scotsman suggested that they hurry on to the Racette home and keep watch to see that Racette and his partner did not escape during the night.

Mathewson finally agreed to keep McLeish company, and the two men rode northward, as the others, who were to join them early the next morning, remained at the hotel. Upon arriving at the Racette house, the two men quietly assumed their positions in the darkness. All was still, although they were sure that at least Racette must be inside, and they waited patiently for dawn.

But, about 1 o'clock, they heard someone stirring within the house. Minutes later, Racette slipped from the doorway and headed for the corral, where he saddled his horse. So far, there had been no sign of his unidentified accomplice and Const. Mathewson, at McLeish's urging, agreed to arrest him before he could get away. Creeping forward, he came up behind the unsuspecting horsethief, grabbed him firmly by the arm and informed him that he was under arrest.

Taken completely by surprise, Racette did not resist, but began to unsaddle his pony. McLeish, who had remained in the shadows, continued to watch the house. When Gaddy, who was unaware that anything was amiss, appeared in the doorway, then headed for the corral, McLeish advanced with drawn gun and ordered him to throw up his hands.

Like Racette, the startled Gaddy offered no resistance. For several long moments the two outlaws stood staring at their captors. The lull ended abruptly when Racette's father, who had been in the house, unknown to either Mathewson or McLeish, slipped from the doorway and crept up on the constable, who was still guarding Racette in the corral. Before Mathewson could handcuff his prisoner, the senior Racette rushed him from behind, leaped on his back and knocked him to the ground, as Racette kicked the gun from the policeman's hand.

When McLeish wheeled about to see what was happening, Gaddy seized the opportunity to leap on Mathewson's revolver, then, turning upon the rancher, he opened fire. The first shot struck McLeish in the side, the second hitting his arm. As McLeish fell, a third bullet buried itself in his back.

Then—incredibly—an eerie peace descended upon the corral, as the outlaws, as stunned by the shooting of McLeish as was Const. Mathewson, agreed to help carry the wounded rancher inside. But the truce did not last long. As the unarmed Mathewson and Racette's father struggled to get McLeish into the house, Gaddy and Racette frantically debated their next step.

Gaddy, who had done the shooting, was adamant that they dispose of the constable, and suggested that Racette agree to accompany the policeman to town for a doctor. Gaddy would wait for them down the road and ambush Mathewson as they rode by. Mathewson, of course, had little choice but to do as they said; particularly as McLeish was in desperate need of medical attention.

The two men then rode towards town, as Gaddy hurried to take up a pre-arranged position. When the riders came abreast of his hiding place, Racette whistled to him to shoot. But, in the darkness, Gaddy was able to see little more than a silhouette and, in his eagerness, shot wild.

Mathewson, spurring his horse, made a rush for Racette, as Gaddy fired twice more. Again he missed, although both shots nicked Mathewson's tunic, when the constable closed with Racette. The frustrated Gaddy then joined the struggle. But, instead of shooting the policeman, he ordered him to go back to the house.

There, the outlaws gathered up their gear and the rest of the stolen horses, warned Mathewson against leaving until they had a good start, and galloped off into the night. They were no sooner out of earshot than the constable began to run towards town, where he aroused Dr. Hutchinson, who quickly accompanied him to the Racette house. After treating McLeish as best he could, Hutchinson had him taken to Pritchard's Hotel. However, for all of his efforts, there was little he could do to save the Scotsman and, later that morning, Hector McLeish died.

Even before the big Scotsman breathed his last, plans were underway for a full-scale manhunt, scores of settlers volunteering to join police in running the killers to earth. Gaddy and Racette had had several hours' headstart, but those in charge of the search did not feel they would go far. With their friends to feed them and hide them out, it was likely that the outlaws would hang about the Crooked Lake reserve. This in mind, the reserve was surrounded and thoroughly searched. But no Gaddy and Racette who, thanks to their friends, were able to slip through the police lines, and make their way south to the border and Montana. Summer passed without a clue as to their whereabouts, the NWMP being unaware that the partners had split up; Racette having gone so far as to take a wife, Gaddy having found a job.

It remained for a travelling photographer to help bring the murderers of Hector McLeish to justice. Months before, two half-breeds had had their pictures taken, then created a scene when photographer Sutherland found they had no money and refused to give them their prints. That fall, the outlaws safely underground in Montana, Sutherland happened to read a belated account of the McLeish slaying, and recognized the murderers by their descriptions as his impoverished customers of the spring. Digging out the photographs, Sutherland hurried straight to His Excellency, Lieutenant-Governor Edgar Dewdney who, upon its being confirmed that the pictures were indeed those of the fugitives, purchased a dozen copies and had them distributed among the NWMP, and across the line among the various lawmen and officials in Montana.

Some weeks elapsed before the Sutherland photographs had any results. When the fugitives were again spotted, it was on the Canadian side of the border. Unfortunately, a hastily-organized posse, although it came close, lost them after two days when the killers again separated. Three more weeks passed. Then the photographs again brought a response. This time, Gaddy and Racette were recognized at Fort McGinnis, Mont., by the Lewiston sheriff who, with with the help of another man, arrested them without a struggle.

When word of their capture was received at NWMP headquarters in Regina, newly-promoted Cpl. Mathewson, a crown prosecutor and a Wolseley settler who knew both wanted men hastened to Montana to make a positive identification. This accomplished, and extradition hearings completed, the outlaws were escorted back to Regina; Insp. Sanders having been warned against letting them escape by Comm. Lawrence Herchmer. If, said Herchmer, it proved to be "impossible to hold them you must shoot them at once, taking care to ensure the necessary evidence in support of your action."

Trial was set for January 10, although this was subsequently postponed in compliance with a defence motion for a sanity hearing for Gaddy. When he was decreed to be of sound mind, the trial opened on February 6. Held at Wolseley, the trial swiftly moved to its inevitable conclusion. When Gaddy's brother, Peter, testified for the crown that he had witnessed the murder of Hector McLeish, the balance of the proceedings were anticlimactic. On February 13, Justice Wetmore passed the death sentence.

To perform the task, Jack Henderson, who had dispatched Louis Riel with admirable efficiency three years before, was engaged by the sheriff. Henderson proceeded to make the arrangements for Gaddy and Racette, who were scheduled to die on June 13, 1888. Upon the condemned men being marched to the scaffold from a second-story window of the police barracks, the part-time hangman gave each man the same eight-foot drop he had allotted Riel. An amateur until he had executed Riel, Henderson had witnessed several hangings while a miner in California, and had volunteered to officiate at the rebel leader's execution to settle a personal grudge that dated back to the Red River uprising. Nevertheless, he had demonstrated his ability in November of 1885.

But James Gaddy and Moise Racette were not Louis Riel. When the trap was sprung, Racette was almost decapitated, although, fortunately for both men, death was swift. And Jack Henderson, the man who hanged Riel, retired from the gruesome profession of executioner.   ●

18

THE DUBOIS GANG

Jack Dubois, an Edmonton newspaper once noted, had had a chequered career on both sides of the 49th parallel. Upon the notorious cattle rustler's being sentenced to five years in prison, the *Journal* pointed out that Dubois had long led the authorities a merry chase:

"In almost every state of the Union his name has been stamped upon the minds of police authorities and time and again he has outwitted the cleverest United States detectives. In Arizona also was he acquitted on a charge of murder arising out of a shooting affray. . . ."

In short, Jack Dubois was quite the fellow. Not only did he transform the precarious pastime of cattle rustling in Alberta into an exact—and highly profitable—science, but he and his gang of cut-throats ruled supreme over almost a thousand square miles of rangeland. When, finally, the authorities succeeded in breaking his stranglehold on this prime cattle country, Jack Dubois had the last laugh.

For years, Dubois, under the name Jim Palmerston, had blazed a path of notoriety across most of the American states, and territories, his most serious offence occurring in Arizona, when he shot a man. Then, having over-stayed his welcome in his own country, he emigrated to Canada; crossing the Montana-Alberta border in mid-1902. With 50 head of cattle, and a respectable nest-egg, the prospective rancher settled near Battle River Valley where, to all outward appearances, he was the model immigrant and rancher.

But Jack Dubois was ambitious and unscrupulous. Before long, his neighbors began to complain of losing more and more head of cattle. Curiously, the only herd unaffected by this wholesale defection was that of Dubois, which, quite to the contrary, grew steadily in size.

Jack was no amateur with a running iron and, recruiting a gang of lawless followers, he continued to prosper. It soon became apparent to the ranchers of the region that he was behind the disappearance of their herds. Time and again, Dubois was charged with cattle theft. Each time he stepped from the courtroom a free man, his record unstained by conviction.

By 1908, Dubois moved his operations to the Hand Hills, 80 miles closer to the border. "Business" continued to prosper. That December, in desperation, the RNWMP, who had been outwitted by the rustler on too many occasions, resolved to break the gang by assigning a single officer to the case. It would be his duty to concentrate solely upon Dubois and company; to monitor their every move, to investigate every reported case of cattle theft, and to do everything possible to link the notorious American with the crimes.

The man chosen for this awesome task was Sgt. Robert W. Ensor, a young Irishman known for his bulldog tenacity. To anyone else, the difficulties of trying to track a gang of expert cattle thieves over a thousand square miles would have been overwhelming. But, to Ensor, the near-impossible was considerably easier to live with than defeat, and he immediately set to work with high hopes—and the four best saddle horses he could find. (Dubois kept a stable of 16 prized horses for his own use).

To say that Sgt. Ensor was alone in the case would not be absolutely correct, as he had the complete support and encouragement of the harrassed ranchers, who were more than eager to give him assistance, information and a change of mount.

Ensor's strategy was to keep a low profile. Wearing plain clothes, and looking like nothing more than a working cowhand, he covered the region to ask questions, take down descriptions of stolen cattle, and to keep tabs on the movements of Jack Dubois and his cronies. At night, he occasionally slipped into the rustling king's herd, looking for the brands of other ranchers, and for signs that brands had been tampered with. When he did find an animal of questionable ownership, he cut it out of the Dubois herd and hid it on a neighboring ranch until enough evidence could be gathered with which to lay a charge.

Throughout the winter of 1908-09, Ensor continued his task.

But he was no longer working alone, as a young English rancher named Henry Brace had joined him in his undercover work; going Ensor one step further by actually joining the Dubois gang. Brace's stake in the game was a personal one. After considerable hard work and hardship, he had acquired a small homestead a hundred miles northeast of Red Deer. But he had no sooner established himself than the Dubois gang ran off his few head of cattle and, in frustration, Brace complained to his fellow stockmen. They were sympathetic but not too encouraging. Too many times, they told "English," the Mounties had attempted to nail Dubois and his gang. Always, the American rustler had walked away. Dissatisfied, to say the least, Brace suggested that they form a delegation and take their complaints straight to the top: the attorney-general. This, they did, the attorney-general passing them on to Supt. Cuthbert, of the NWMP.

Cuthbert again outlined the difficulties of proving a case against the rustlers. Then he proposed that one of their members infiltrate the gang and act as contact to the force's own man in the field, Sgt. Ensor. Henry Brace the youngest of the stockmen, and unmarried, was nominated for the role.

He promptly set out to win the friendship, then the confidence, of Jack Dubois. Only once, he recalled many years afterward, did the cattle rustler act as though he suspected the latest addition to the gang. This occurred when Dubois happened to see him rounding up some calves. Brace had not told him that he had worked as a cowpuncher for Pat Burns, the meat packer, having played the part of a greenhorn. For a split second he had seen the suspicion in Dubois' eyes as he observed Brace's skill with horse and rope. Then the outlaw leader smiled, and complimented him for having mastered cowpunching so quickly.

As a member of the gang, Brace was able to learn considerably more than the indefatigable Ensor could possibly hope to achieve by working from the outside. When the gang ran herds of stolen cattle back and forth across the border, Henry Brace was with them. In this manner he was able to discover the identities of most of the gang members, such as the Holts and the Solways, and those of their business contacts on both sides of the line. For Dubois, it would seem, had grown cocky over the six years he had been in operation; a fact which made both Brace's and Ensor's work somewhat easier. Before long, Brace had learned the full extent of the Dubois empire, which covered not only southern Alberta and northern Montana, but part of Idaho as well.

By the end of March, 1909, Ensor felt he had sufficient

evidence with which to go to trial. On the morning of the 25th, he donned his sergeant's uniform and with two other officers, and six warrants, headed for the Holt ranch at Battle River. During the day-long ride, Ensor had ample time in which to contemplate the future. Both of the Holt brothers were known as hardcases, Irven having served five years in Idaho for horse theft, and could be expected to resist arrest. But, when the three Mounties charged into the ranchyard at dusk, the Holts were caught unawares and surrendered without a fight. They were taken to the nearest community and locked overnight in the post office, as Ensor and his fellow officers went in search of the others on their list.

With daybreak, they arrested three more of Dubois' lieutenants, Joe Cardinal, and the Solways, Abe and Louis, and escorted them to Stettler. That done, Ensor would personally serve the warrant on Dubois.

But, at Stettler, the Mountie was informed that Dubois, having heard of the arrests of his men, had fled. Ensor promptly ordered two policemen to keep watch on Dubois' ranch, reasoning that the rustler would show up there sooner or later. But Dubois did not return to the Hand Hills. Rather, he boarded a train for Calgary where, the Mounties having learned of his plans, arrested him in the office of the noted lawyer, Paddy Nolan.

Sixteen days after Sgt. Ensor began his sweep, Jack Dubois was returned to Stettler.

But Ensor was not about to rest. Well aware that his case against Dubois was, at best, a legalistic house of cards, he had determined to reinforce his evidence by pinning the rustler to every single crime that he could uncover. Dubois, in his opinion, was the worst professional cattle thief that had ever stolen a head of beef in that country.

With Dubois, the acknowledged head and brains of the gang, in jail, Ensor and his fellow officers continued their investigation; even taking clippers to each head of cattle seized on the Dubois and Holt spreads, when cattlemen who had lost their beef were invited to examine the brands. Of the almost 400 animals examined, several were positively identified by the ranchers as having come from their herds.

Then began the legal battles. Dubois, who was to spend more than $20,000 for his defence, and who was known to have three times as much salted away, was able to delay the crown prosecutors from the beginning. His cronies, not as well-heeled, and lacking his influence, were not as fortunate and, one by one, with the exception of Abe Solway, tumbled to Ensor's evidence. Joe Cardinal got off with a mere three months, Jim Holt with two years in the penitentiary at Edmonton. Brother Irven, who had once received a 12-year sentence in Idaho, fell for nine years.

With the best legal expense money could buy, Dubois, the onetime American badman, successfully eluded the crown's net as charge after charge was dismissed for lack of evidence. Months passed as the case dragged on in the courts; the time-consuming and expensive skirmishing even draining the provincial budget.

For Sgt. Ensor, Dubois' successful defiance of the crown's charges were all the more galling as he had invested months of painstaking work in building his case. When the judge dismissed the charges on the grounds that ownership of the animals had not been proved, the crown appealed. The Supreme Court overruled the lower court, and a new trial was ordered, when the battle was fought anew. This time, however, Dubois was sentenced to five years at hard labor on each charge, the terms to run concurrently.

Taken to Fort Saskatchewan, Dubois served nine months while his lawyers launched an appeal. This time, he won the round, the court having accepted his argument that the animals in question had been branded mistakenly by his son and without his knowledge.

Although most of the victimized cattlemen were outraged at this final outcome, the threat of the Dubois gang was forever removed. Most of the gang had fled the country the moment Sgt. Ensor had begun the arrests of the ringleaders. Those convicted also headed for greener pastures upon completion of their sentences. With Jack Dubois' departure for British Columbia, a relieved rancher exclaimed that Alberta was at last rid of a "pest worse than mange!"   •

19

FRANK SPENCER

Morning, July 21, 1890, broke bright and clear.

For some time the little town of Kamloops continued to sleep soundly. Then an occasional column of smoke indicated that early risers were preparing for breakfast, and another day had begun.

As far as 36-year-old Frank Spencer was concerned, morning had come all too soon. As he nervously paced his cell, the light outside his window steadily brightened. For hours, he had hobbled back and forth, dragging his leg irons, unable to sleep. When a guard quietly asked what he wanted for breakfast, he asked only for a cup of tea.

Then the metallic click of a key in the lock told him that his first visitors had arrived, when, with a relieved smile, he greeted the two berobed figures. A third visitor was not as welcome; jailer Sinclair having arrived, hammer and cold chisel in hand, to remove the leg irons. Then all waited impatiently for the ringing of steel to cease.

Minutes later, Sinclair was finished, and two late-comers joined those in the crowded cell. Spencer, looking out the window, stared, fascinated, at the gangling wooden structure to which workmen had just given the finishing touches. Then, with a slight shudder, he turned to the others.

It was time to go.

As noted, July 21, 1890, had arrived with terrifying

suddenness for Spencer. But those who knew him, and of his career below the 49th parallel, could only marvel that his date with eternity had been so long in coming. For violence was no stranger to the lanky Tennesseean. During 20 of his 36 years, he had been involved in one scrape after another, having drifted with fortune's tide throughout the American southwest since the age of 16.

By the time of his arrival in British Columbia's Similkameen Valley, in 1886, the Tennessee cowboy could boast of having known Dodge City in its riproaring heyday, and such illuminaries as Wyatt Earp and Bat Masterson. In Tombstone he had ridden with the Clanton brothers; at least until their ill-fated encounter with Earp and Doc Holliday in the O.K. Corral. Then it was on to Colorado, Montana, and the future province of Alberta; the latter step, Spencer's first outside the United States, being but one ahead of vigilantes fed up with his handiwork with a branding iron.

After a stretch as a cowhand, Spencer headed westward once more; this time to the boom town of Kamloops, in the summer of 1886. Despite the differences between the free and easy towns below the border and Kamloops, then bursting with expectations for a prosperous future, Spencer seems to have found it to his liking and he found work as a cowhand on the Campbell Ranch, 10 miles east of town. Throughout the wicked winter of '86, the retired gunman and rustler kept his nose clean; except on paydays, when he would drown the past in cheap liquor in a Kamloops saloon, or in the Campbell bunkhouse.

This seems to have been the lifestyle for his fellow ranch hands as well. Besides sharing their jobs and quarters, they also shared the occasional bottle; a cameraderie which ended with sudden violence on the evening of May 20, 1887.

That Friday, Spencer was going into town and Pete Foster, a 22-year-old French Canadian, handed him five dollars with the request that he bring back four bottles of whisky. To this, Spencer agreed and, later that day, he headed back to the Campbell ranch with Foster's order. He did not go far before the Tennessee badman was struck by the thought that such a favor was worth a small commission. This in mind, he pulled the cork from a bottle and tilted it to his lips.

By the time he reached the ranch, Spencer was feeling no pain, and the opened bottle was almost consumed. When Foster met him at the corral, eager to receive his shipment, Spencer handed him the three full bottles and casually waved the empty as notice of his having taken his "share."

Foster was furious. He worked damn hard for his money.

Who the hell did Spencer think he was, drinking his whisky?

Voice rising, Foster demanded restitution. Spencer responded with a shrug and continued to unsaddle his horse. With an oath, Foster seized him by the shoulder, spun him around, and lashed out with his fist. The blow sent Spencer reeling against the fence, where he quickly caught himself and regained his feet. As the young Montrealer closed in, Spencer reached desperately for an equalizer. In all of his years below the line, he had done his fighting with pistol, rifle and knife, and he was not about to change his style now; particularly as Foster would likely beat him to a pulp.

Grabbing the knife from his belt, he faced his antagonist with renewed confidence. But Foster, as angry as he was, was not intent upon committing suicide. When he turned to run, Spencer took off after him. Foster, however, had little difficulty in eluding him.

Spencer soon gave up the chase and Foster, thinking the incident over, returned to the bunkhouse. He did not realize that Spencer, fired with cheap whisky and the "code of the West," was determined to settle the matter the way they did in Dodge City and Tombstone. Hurrying into Campbell's house, he snatched his employer's Winchester from the wall and charged outside.

Foster, upon spotting the rifle, began to run for cover—just as Spencer levered a round into the breech, snapped the rifle to his shoulder and, with the speed and motion of a man long used to such situations, fired at the running figure. The .44 calibre slug penetrated Fraser's right arm, passed through his stomach and lodged in his left side, spinning him to the ground before any of the horrified ranch hands could move to stop him.

Almost by reflex, Spencer headed for the stable at a run, as the others raced to Foster's aid. Once inside, Spencer saddled his employer's fastest bay and led it into the yard. Then, leaping into the saddle, he waved the stolen Winchester, cautioned the others that he might use it again, and rode away.

But the others were more concerned with getting Foster to hospital. Even before the gunman was out of sight, they were harnessing a team and wagon and preparing the wounded man for the long ride to town. When they finally reached the hospital, Dr. Tunstall removed the bullet. But Foster's condition steadily worsened and, at 4 o'clock the next morning, he died.

The body was still warm when the inquest was opened in the Kamloops court house. The verdict was as promptly delivered: "That Pete Foster came to his death by means of a rifle ball, shot from a rifle in the hands of Frank Spencer and that he (Spencer) is guilty of wilful murder."

Despite the determined efforts of provincial police and Indian trackers, Spencer easily eluded pursuit. Keeping off the main trails and camping without a fire, he worked his way south towards the Washington border. A week after shooting Foster, he crossed the line.

Five weeks after he vanished, his former employer wanted his horse back and advertised to this effect in the Kamloops *Sentinel*:

STOLEN! FROM L. CAMPBELL'S RANCH

By Frank Spencer, a horse, saddle and bridle; and a .44 calibre Winchester repeating rifle. The horse was a bay, with part of its forehead white, and branded Lc on the left shoulder; the saddle was of California make, double cinsh, and block stirrup; narrow; the bridle had hand made reins and snaffle bit. Anyone delivering the same to the undersigned at Kamloops will be suitably rewarded.

L. CAMPBELL, June 25, 1887.

But Campbell's horse was not to be found—and neither was Frank Spencer. Safe on American soil, he vanished. In actual fact, he had gone only as far as the Snake River country of Washington, then Oregon, where he again worked as a cowhand. Two years passed without a word of the Kamloops killer and B.C. Provincial Police, although they had not forgotten him, gave less and less attention to the yellowing wanted circulars, as more pressing cases developed.

And on that unsatisfactory note the Frank Spencer case might well have ended—had he not pressed his luck one last time. In the spring of 1889, Spencer again headed for the Canadian border.

This time, he was one of a number of cowboys escorting a herd of horses to New Westminster for an Oregon rancher. When, days after, their steamer docked at the Royal City, the cowboys herded their charges ashore and were paid off. Within minutes of receiving their money, they were headed for the nearest saloons; Spencer fingering the bills in his pocket and looking forward to some relaxation before heading back across the border.

For days, he haunted the bars lining Columbia Street, as his money dwindled. With elbows on the bar, and a bottle before him, he did not notice the policeman who entered the saloon and pushed his way through the crowd. Then Sgt. McLaren, in firm voice, and with hand on the drinker's shoulder, told him that he was under arrest. Spencer was struck dumb with amazement. It had never occurred to him that he might be recognized in New Westminster. Yet here was this policeman, snapping handcuffs on his wrists and leading him away. Out in the street and on their way to jail, Spencer could do little more than protest that it was a case of mistaken identity.

That fall, a preliminary hearing was held before Kamloops justice of the peace, James McIntosh, with W.W. Spinks prosecuting for the crown, W. H. Whittaker appearing for the defence. The first day lasted three and a half hours, with eight witnesses formally identifying the prisoner as Frank Spencer. Then the hearing was remanded until other witnesses could get to town. Spencer was returned to his cell, where a reporter from the *Inland Sentinel*, who obviously knew nothing of his career as an outlaw, described him as "yet comparatively speaking, a young man. He does not present the appearance of a man who would commit so serious a crime as that with which he is charged."

Bound over to the spring assizes of 1890, Spencer was duly convicted of Foster's murder and given over to the care of jailer Sinclair. Then the days fled by all too swiftly, and it was morning of July 21, 1890.

The last hours were the longest. Spencer, unable to sleep at the end, ignored his leg irons to pace his 60-square-foot cell. Then, with the arrival of his two spiritual advisors, the removal of the irons by Sinclair, and the arrival of Sheriff Pemberton and Fred Hussey of the provincial police, the death procession was formed. As they prepared to leave the cell, Spencer made a last request. In a final symbolic gesture to the wild and woolly west of his past, he asked for a pair of slippers; explaining that he did not wish to die with his boots on. These were immediately brought and Spencer, having overcome his nervousness of the night, stepped firmly towards the scaffold, mounted the steps, took his position on the trap, and shook hands with all but his black-hooded executioner.

The hangman adjusted the noose and put the white hood in place, as Spencer mumbled a prayer. When the Tennessee outlaw finished, he was seen to tremble slightly and Sheriff Pemberton nodded to the executioner, who let the trap drop. Death was said to have been instantaneous and, as a final note in the career of Frank Spencer, a Kamloops correspondent noted that the hangman, who had worn a hood so as to conceal his identity, was from Victoria and well-known.   •

20

BULLDOG KELLY

It would take little less than a full-fledged miracle to uncover a murderer's loot cached near the town of Golden, British Columbia, but if a treasure hunter could match painstaking research with phenomenal luck, he might find himself $4,500 richer.

This is the money stolen in a wild robbery over 90 years ago; a rip-roaring gun battle whose shots resounded from the wilds of B.C. to the national capitals of Canada and the U.S. When the smoke cleared—six years later—history finally drew the curtain on one of the most unusual criminal cases in provincial record.

It was 24 miles south of Golden, where Kootenay trail shouldered Kicking Horse River, on the chill morning of Nov. 27, 1884, that our strange tale of murder and lost treasure began.

In the half-light of dawn, three horsemen picked their way, single file, through snowdrifts which covered the narrow, winding trail. Leading was a young man named Manvel Drainard, followed by well-known Montana liquor salesman Robert McGregor Baird. Popularly known as Harold Baird, the American was returning to Missoula, Mont., with his season's receipts for Eddy, Hammond & Co. It had been a good trip; in his bulging pocket and saddlebag was $4,500 in gold and currency.

Bringing up the rear was his packer and guide, a half-breed named Harry.

The trio continued southward at a slow but steady gait. It was as they navigated a wider stretch in the trail that tragedy struck. Baird was halfway across when, without warning, a shot punctured the stillness. The heavy ball caught him square in the chest, spinning him, lifeless, from the saddle. Taken completely by surprise, Drainard snapped a frightened look back, saw Baird pitch to the ground, then spurred his mount. Unarmed and totally unnerved, his only thought was to get beyond range. The terrified youth charged off down the trail, leaving hapless Harry with a corpse—and a hidden killer.

Glancing wildly about, Harry spotted the sniper just as he fired again. A solid wall of white-hot pain slammed the packer as the bullet tore into his hip. The concussion almost knocked him from his saddle but, regaining his balance, the courageous half-breed jerked his rifle from its scabbard, levered a shell into the breech and fired, all in the same motion.

His shot whistled harmlessly into the trees as the startled killer snapped off a third round, which also missed. Before either could reload, Harry had closed with the stranger. The frightened horses collided, squealing, riders savagely jousting with empty rifles. His wound forgotten in the heat of battle, Harry leaped onto the murderer, both men crashing heavily to the ground.

Then—despite his shattered hip—Harry grappled with the unknown antagonist for almost 15 minutes. But he was bleeding badly. Unable to land a solid blow in the wild scuffle, time was running out for the heroic guide. Making the struggle even more one-sided was the fact his opponent proved to be of extraordinary strength and stamina.

Finally, it was over. Overcome by loss of blood and shock, Harry slumped to the trail, unconscious. To make sure he would be no further trouble, the exhausted assassin delivered several fierce kicks to the fallen man's head, then staggered to his horse to catch his breath.

When Harry came to, he was alone. Carefully easing himself to his feet, he surveyed the grim scene dizzily. It took several seconds before his reeling senses cleared enough for him to observe the killer's handiwork. Baird lay in the mud where he had fallen, almost naked. The highwayman had methodically slashed open his clothing, even removing boots and socks. Nearby, Baird's horse grazed quietly, freed of saddlebags. These too had been slashed apart and ransacked.

But Harry was not thinking of the missing money. He had just enough strength to clamber into the saddle and knee the animal toward Kicking Horse, booming construction camp of the building Canadian Pacific Railway. It was nightfall when the battered guide arrived. He was almost unconscious, eyes and mouth swollen shut, teeth caked in dried blood. Somehow he managed to mumble details of Baird's murder. As someone ran for medical assistance, Harry mustered his last surge of will power to describe the killer, then passed out.

In the meantime, young Drainard had been busy also. Panic-stricken when the killer had started blazing away from the trees, he had galloped several miles down the trail before reining his lathered horse. For long minutes, the youth debated his course of action. Should he hurry to Golden for help or return to the others? He had no gun...was probably too scared to use one anyway.

At last he decided. Squaring his shoulders, Drainard wheeled his horse about and galloped back to his companions, arriving minutes after Harry had begun his painful ride to Kicking Horse. Upon seeing that Baird was dead, and not knowing what had become of Harry, Drainard hurried to Golden with the news.

At Kicking Horse, the manhunt was already underway, outraged construction workers eagerly volunteering to join the posses being formed by Northwest Mounted and Provincial Police officers. The angry posses fanned out from Golden and Kicking Horse, combing every ravine, every creekbed, every goat track that might offer an escape to the murderer.

Telegraph keys chattered noisily from Victoria, provincial capital, to Winnipeg, Manitoba, as the details of the cold-blooded killing and Harry's description of the slayer were distributed to all law enforcement agencies. The hunt became even more active when the Montana firm which had employed Baird offered a reward of $1,000, to which the province added $250. Everywhere, hundreds of probing eyes carefully scrutinized all strangers—even friends—for a man "about five feet 11 inches in height...blue eyes, mustache of a light color, turned up at the ends, reddish complexion, and chin whiskers apparently cut with scissors...dark suit, sack coat and Scotch cap with peak."

Police had already put a name to the description: "Bulldog" Kelly, a loudmouthed, redhaired American of questionable employment who had been drifting about the Kootenays for about a year.

But of Kelly himself there was not a trace. It was a big, rugged country, and he had vanished like a ghost. Even Indian trackers had little success following the signs left at the murder scene. The single, solid clue they found was the

murder weapon; Kelly had dropped or thrown the rifle into
Kicking Horse River.

Police received a report that Bulldog was in Golden but a
thorough search of the town and vicinity failed to yield a sign
of the wanted man. Kootenay Gold Commissioner Vowell
dispatched two more constables to assist the investigation at
Kicking Horse.

Days later, the search had slowed to a frustrating crawl.
Scant clues were forthcoming; it looked like Bulldog had made
good his escape to the American side. Then, whether acting on
a hunch or on information suddenly come to hand, one of the
officers decided to have the Winnipeg bound train searched.
Firing off a telegram to a water stop ahead of the train, he
asked the crew to check its passengers for Kelly, without, if
possible, arousing his suspicions if he was aboard.

Coincidentally, among the passengers were two qualified to
act upon the request: none other than Col. A.G. Irvine and
Col. McLeod of the NWMP. The telegram gave a brief outline of
Baird's slaying and Kelly's description. Colonels Irvine and
McLeod decided it was a good time to stretch their legs and
separated.

Irvine spotted him first. Dressed in the rough garb of a
railway worker, the redhaired suspect was watching the vast
praireland sweep by his dust-streaked window. Irvine strolled
through the car, seemingly preoccupied with his own thoughts,
passed the stranger, then paused at the end of the car. This
was Kelly, he was sure. Without glancing back, he decided to
arrest him then and there rather than wait for McLeod.

When Irvine turned—the man was gone. The alarmed
officer strode to the door, jerked it open and stepped onto the
platform. He almost collided with Kelly, who was leaning
against the railing. Just as Irvine "put out his hand to arrest
him..." reported the Victoria *Daily Colonist*, "the man LEAPED
FROM THE TRAIN, which was not running at a very rapid
rate. He was not injured, and the moment he regained his feet
he ran for dear life across the plains."

Irvine instantly yanked the emergency cord, the train
screeching to a halt moments later. But of Kelly there was not a
sign. The Mounties had no choice but to return to the train and
telegraph the news to all detachments from the next station.

Days, weeks...months passed, without another clue as to
Kelly's whereabouts. That he would return to the U.S.
Canadian authorities were positive. They concentrated their
search by circular, giving his description to law enforcement
agencies as far south as Oregon, as far east as Minnesota.

Baird had been buried almost eight months when provincial

constable Jack Kirkup of Revelstoke found Kelly. Working on
special orders from Victoria, with permission of Minnesota
authorities, Kirkup finally traced the wily suspect to Crook-
stone. Once he had found Kelly, it was an easy matter to have
him arrested by local marshals.

And that, thought Kirkup, was that. A brief extradition
hearing, then Kelly would be enroute to B.C. in irons to stand
trial.

If only Kirkup could have known!

For our dear Mr. Kelly, it seems, was not just an ordinary
desperado. He had friends. Important friends. And when they
were through pulling strings, creating smokescreens and
calling names, B.C. authorities were sorry they had ever
heard of the leering Irishman.

Despite the able and determined efforts of Deputy Attorney-
General Paulus Aemilius Irving, assisted by Const. W. McNeill,
provincial authorities were stalled at every turn by Kelly's
influential allies. It took seven bitter, aggravating months for
the Canadians to even bring Kelly before U.S. Commissioner
Spencer in St. Paul. Mr. Irving, used to the more polished ways
of British Justice, could not understand the American lack of
co-operation and sympathy. After all, Kelly was charged with
murdering an American. And didn't B.C. offer concrete
evidence and concrete witnesses, such as Harry, the guide?

However, despite their every effort, Kelly's friends could not
damage Harry's testimony. Commissioner Spencer ordered
Kelly surrendered to the Canadians.

Undaunted, Kelly's lawyer "Big Tom" Ryan caught the next
train to Washington, D.C. His intention: Nothing less than a
meeting with the Secretary of State Thomas F. Bayard! The
new strategy worked; another month dragged by, Ryan's deft
manoeuvring stalling every move the Canadians made.

Raged the Victoria *Colonist*: "The refusal of Washington
authorities to make the order for the extradition of Bulldog
Kelly does certainly not indicate the existence of that
reciprocal feeling which the province has always manifested
in assisting the U.S. to bring fugitive criminals to justice.

"In no civilized country is the laxity of its laws so noticeable
as in the U.S., where the law's delays too often end in their
final evasion. Whether the prisoner Kelly is innocent or guilty,
it is evident to all those who have read copies of the deposition
of witnesses in the case that there is ample ground to warrant
the order for the prisoner's extradition. The fine scrupulous-
ness displayed in this instance by the American authorities
would almost incline one to the belief that extradition on a
charge of murder to B.C. meant the prisoner's subsequent

conviction of the crime.

"The attitude of the province in these matters displays a striking contrast to that of its powerful neighbor. Our local governments have invariably proved themselves as indefatigable in detecting and arresting extraditable fugitives from the states as if the law had been outraged in our own country; thereby observing the true spirit of the treaty—to expedite the administration of justice apart from the consideration in which of the two countries that justice was contravened."

The editors drew scathing attention to the case of a murderer named Morgan, who had been swiftly handed over to the U.S. Which was as good a time as any to draw Montana's attention to the fact it still owed B.C. for legal costs!

The editorial concluded with the final remonstration, "...It would be well for (U.S. authorities) to ... recognize the rights belonging to Canada as a party to the existing treaty, and facilitate, not obstruct, a country whose only fault (?) may be that in the administration of justice she is more tenacious in effort, a lesser respector of persons, quicker to try, as slow to condemn, and swifter to execute than any other constitutional government on the American continent."

Finally Washington was moved to action; but not of the kind B.C. was hoping for. Instead, convinced by Ryan's gilt arguments, the extradition order was quashed! Stunned but not beaten, Mr. Irving's squad immediately countered with another affidavit, this time that of Manvel Drainard.

Once again, the Canadians went before Commissioner Spencer, and once again he heard Ryan's tirades and writs of habeas corpus. And once again the weary commissioner accepted B.C.'s case, committing Kelly for extradition. Jubilant with victory at last, Irving and his witnesses headed home, leaving the constables to follow with the prisoner.

This time it had been Ryan's turn to express amazement. He and his two colleagues had constructed what he considered a perfect battery of nine defence witnesses—"four to prove an alibi and five to impeach the veracity of the witnesses for the Crown.

"These witnesses for the defence had been, in November, 1884, engaged on the construction of the CPR, and in Kootenay district it would have been easy to show the reputations they had earned for themselves, but at St. Paul it was not open for the prosecution to do so. All the prosecution could do was to show by the inconsistencies in their evidence that their story was not worthy of credence. This was undertaken by the prosecution, and, as the commissioner has committed the prisoner, we may presume it was attended with success."

The *Colonist* ended with a last complaint: "The proceedings
were conducted with a licence that would not be tolerated in a
magistrate's court in this country—the prisoner enjoying a
cigar and conversing with his many sympathizers."

But, "towards the close of the case, it was evident that the
long strain on his nervous system was beginning to tell, and
once the court had to adjourn on account of his ill health."

Then, for B.C., disaster. Ryan returned from a second visit to
Washington with a final decision—from President Grover
Cleveland himself. It was a long story of backroom politics.
Apparently Ryan had told the president of Kelly's past good
work for the Minnesota Democratic Party. Not to mention the
fact he was as Irish as the Blarney Stone.

At that time, when rebellion raged in Ireland, the Emerald
Isle population of the U.S. had a loud, strong voice election-
wise. And they backed compatriot Kelly to a man. It would be
politically unwise, advised Ryan, if Kelly were turned over to
the barbarous British in Canada.

The Irish might not have been so loyal to Kelly had they
known he was born Edward Loughlin—in Illinois!

At least this was the devious plotting as deduced by angry
British Columbia.

Whatever, Kelly was now a free man.

Said the Bulldog: "It is good news...I have no idea as to
whether the Canadian authorities will carry the matter
further, but I don't propose to stand any more of it. It is a
persecution of the worst kind, and ought to stop right here. I've
been in confinement eight months for nothing, as the decision
shows. The stories of my being well supplied with money are
not true. I had $10 when I was arrested, and with the exception
of $100 paid Mr. Steenerson for me, that is all the lawyers have
received for my case. If the Canadian authorities push it
further, I'll bring up stronger evidence than shown yet."

Moaned the *Colonist*: "Money and political influence have
been too potent, and Kelly is now treading the firm soil and
breathing the pure air of a country where all are free—free to
make justice a travesty, to treat murder as a joke, and to turn a
criminal trial and sentence into a mockery—if they do but
possess the subtle key to the necessary mechanism...

"Kelly may be legally free, but he goes forth with a red stain
on his conscience, if he has any, and with a liberty that is
conditional upon his never placing his feet upon British soil.
Until then his crime rests between himself and his Maker. As it
is, the U.S. is responsible...for prostituting its freedom by
wrapping its flag around the body of a prima facie
murderer..."

The St. Paul *Irish Standard* editorialized back: "Kelly, the accused, remained for a considerable time in the northwest after the murder, unmolested, and it was not until he had crossed the line into the U.S. that the bloodhounds of the so-called British justice, true to the instincts of their bloodthirsty ancestors, came in pursuit, endeavoring to trample down every vestige of justice and fair play in our midst, and drag the object of their enmity again into their kennels and consign him, as many an honest Irishman has been consigned before, to an ignominious death on the scaffold whose bloodstains, like the blood of Abel, cry aloud for vengeance on the cowardly curs who have so often besmeared it with the heart's blood of the bravest and true. The Canadian government has already spent $30,000 on the case through the instrumentality of a corduroyed, tight pants dude of a lawyer they sent here, who knew well that the guilty party was not Kelly."

Whew!

Bulldog Kelly drifted back into anonymity for the next two years. His name again graced newspapers from Minnesota to B.C. when it was reported, in January, 1888, that he had been lynched for unstated activities in Colorado. This, however, was but "a case of somebody having been 'stuffed,' as Kelly is leading a peaceful and Christian life in Massachusetts."

But even Kelly's powerful friends could not save him from ultimately standing before a greater bar of justice—fate. In April, 1890, he was working as a brakeman on the North Pacific Railway. One afternoon as the freight slowed to enter Helena, Kelly ran along the cars to his post. Suddenly, with a scream, he tripped and fell between two cars.

Unlike his leap to freedom from another train, six years before, this was the end. When his comrades rushed back to him, he was alive but beyond help. Both legs had been crushed below the knees and he died on the operating table. Death had come to Bulldog Kelly, onetime terror of the Kootenays.

And the $4,500? Just minutes before the accident, Kelly had been chatting with his crewmen in the caboose. He had mentioned retirement; this was his last trip. After Helena, he was heading to British Columbia, where he would come into some money. And he winked at the others.

Kelly faced a hangman's noose if he set foot in B.C. Which meant he must have cached the loot under a log or rock in the Kootenays back in '84. And there it must be today, if time and weather have not disposed of it, awaiting some lucky treasure hunter. But as the police had grimly observed when chasing Kelly so many years ago: It's a big country, and rugged.

Even today, civilization has made few major changes to the

mountainous Kootenays. With few minor exceptions, it is much like the wilderness Kelly knew when outrunning the posse. If anyone is interested in chasing down this lost hoard, we'd like to wish them good luck. They'll need it! •

BIBLIOGRAPHY:
B.C. Provincial Archives; Ashcroft *Journal;* *Shoulder Strap;* Victoria *Daily Times; British Columbian; Inland Sentinel;* Vernon *News;* Vancouver *Province: Sun;* Merritt *Herald;* Public Archives of Canada; The *Victorian;* Cumberland Museum; *Maintain the Right,* by Ronald Atkin (Macmillan); *The Royal Canadian Mounted Police,* by Nora and William Kelly (Hurtig); *Pictorial History of the RCMP,* by S.W. Horrall (McGraw-Hill Ryerson). Special acknowledgement to the editors of *Real West* magazine for permission to reprint articles which have appeared in that popular American publication.

PHOTOGRAPHS:
The author thanks the following agencies and individuals for the use of photos found in this book: B.C. Government, B.C. Provincial Archives, B.C. Provincial Museum, Cumberland Museum, Duck Lake Museum, V.C. Friesen, Glenbow Foundation, Public Archives of Canada, and Saskatchewan Archives.